Affirmations for Self-Love

100 Lessons for Learning to Love Yourself Through the Beautiful Days, the Hard Days, and Everything in Between

ZANNA KEITHLEY

ADAMS MEDIA
NEW YORK AMSTERDAM/ANTWERP LONDON TORONTO
SYDNEY/MELBOURNE NEW DELHI

For the ones who have chosen the path less traveled and have persevered through adversity with incredible strength, resilience, and grace—you are seen, you are loved, and you are never alone.

Adams Media
An Imprint of Simon & Schuster, LLC
100 Technology Center Drive
Stoughton, MA 02072

First Adams Media hardcover edition September 2025

Interior design by Maya Caspi

Manufactured in the United States of America

1 2025

Library of Congress Control Number: 2025940135

ISBN 978-1-5072-2434-2
ISBN 978-1-5072-2435-9 (ebook)

Contents

The Affirmations

Introduction

When you recite a positive affirmation like *I am worthy*, you're not *becoming* worthy. You're remembering your own innate, inextricable worthiness. When you boldly claim *I am unstoppable*, you are uncovering that once-hidden, beautiful truth. When you affirm *I am compassionate*, that inner love radiates. Regardless of the affirmation, by speaking it, you are unearthing it from inside yourself—pulling it back up through the layers of limiting beliefs and false stories you've accumulated over the years and reconnecting with the core of who you truly are.

In *Affirmations for Self-Love*, you'll find one hundred positive affirmations for loving yourself; you'll embrace the beautiful spirit and talent you have within that will guide you in appreciating the person you are now and who you want to become. Each affirmation is a sentence or two long, and each is accompanied by a revelatory message that dives deeper into the heart of the words to help you access the central feeling behind the affirmation.

View these longer messages as meditations and lessons to help you reconnect with your true self, the very essence of who you already are, deep inside. Let the affirmations and messages together speak self-love into your heart and empower you through your life's beautiful seasons—times when the seeds of love, joy, and success bloom into something more incredible than you had ever imagined.

In these seasons, the words on these pages will help you receive what's meant for you with an open heart—and silence any self-doubt coming from your innermost thoughts.

Let your self-love affirmations be your strength through your hard seasons, when the world feels heavy and even small tasks seem impossible, when you're not sure what to do or where to go or what your purpose is anymore. During these times, these words will gently guide you through your dark hours.

Let your affirmations guide you through the in-between seasons of contraction and expansion, through the seasons of pursuing your dreams, and through the seasons of pursuing yourself.

Through every season of your self-love journey, the words in this book will guide you to stay true to your authentic self, honor your heart's inner wisdom, and forever walk your sacred path with the companionship of your own deep, enduring love.

This book is not for becoming someone or something that you are not.

This book is for remembering all that you are—for reconnecting with who you were always meant to be.

How to Use This Book

Affirmations for Self-Love is designed to support your lifelong journey of embracing your every facet. Within these pages, there are affirmations for cultivating self-belief, trusting your intuition, following your heart's true calling, embracing gratitude, aligning with the energy of joy and abundance, and embracing your authentic self. This book can be used as part of your daily self-care practice, and you may also choose to reach for it in moments of need to receive loving guidance and support.

Ultimately, you are empowered to choose how you want to interact with these pages and use them in a way that best serves your mind, body, and soul. Later in this section, you'll find suggestions for how to choose your affirmations and incorporate them into your daily routine, but first, to get the most out of the self-love affirmations, it's important to understand what they are and how to best use them, so that you can rely on them throughout your compassionate self-growth journey.

What Are Affirmations for Self-Love?

A positive affirmation is a short, first-person statement that is designed to uplift, encourage, and boost your confidence and self-belief. In a general sense, affirmations are powerful statements written in the present tense and should be used to help you in the areas of your life you wish to improve.

Self-love is the unflinching loyalty and compassion given to yourself from yourself. It's appreciating your current, past, and future selves and what you have to offer the world around you. So, ultimately, combining affirmations with self-love brings forth self-confidence and inner peace. Using self-love-focused affirmations uncovers inner truths and strengths you may have forgotten in the chaos of everyday life. For example, when feeling scared or unsure, proclaiming *I am brave* would be helpful in recapturing your courageous nature. Or, switching subjects, declare *I am loved* when you feel lonely. These empowering words can help you to maintain a sense of stability when the world around you feels shaky and uncertain.

Cultivate Self-Love Through Affirmations

With these self-love affirmations, you get to choose the narrative you consciously cultivate for yourself. You decide your own beliefs and perspectives and who you want to be in each moment. Essentially, you create your present-day experience and the story you tell about your life through your mindful, chosen thoughts.

For instance, in the past, when you were confronted with obstacles and challenges, your frustration may have resulted in short outbursts or closing yourself off from others. But by consistently using self-love affirmations, you can train your brain to remain calm when a roadblock shows up on your path. This mindful thinking allows you to see the situation more clearly and regulate your emotions so that you don't respond from a state of stress or fear but instead honor your ability to give love to yourself and those outside of yourself.

After learning more about how you want to practice your self-love, when a challenge arises, you might affirm *I am always capable of handling anything that comes my way*. You might affirm *I have what it takes to walk through life's harshest storms with incredible strength and grace*. You might even affirm *All obstacles offer hidden opportunities* when you're willing to look a little deeper at what each experience is trying to show you. These simple sentences can change your entire outlook and way of life.

The Importance of Daily Self-Love Affirmations

Self-love affirmations are the key to creating a rich, beautiful, and fulfilling life. When you use affirmations every day to embrace who you are now and who you want to be, you will notice the profound effect they have on every facet of your life.

First, as you begin to use daily affirmations, you'll notice a positive shift in your overarching mindset. Your inner and outer worlds are constantly changing. Some mornings, you wake up feeling fresh and excited for the day, and other times it feels impossible to pull yourself out of your bad mood. But affirmations give you the power to make the impossible possible. Even on your most stressful mornings, you can still affirm that you are competent, confident, and capable. This ability to shift into a calmer, more positive headspace ensures that no matter what is happening within or around you, you remain connected with your soul's deepest truth and with the love you've cultivated within.

Using affirmations every day doesn't just shift your mindset; in time, you'll find that it transforms every aspect of your life. With powerful self-love affirmations, you can speak your desired world into existence every day and measure your progress on the road to that world with consistent reflection. These uplifting statements guide you to a positive, more inquisitive and connected way to live your life and love yourself today. Plus, they can reconnect you with the deep-rooted wisdom that lives inside your heart so that you feel empowered to trust your intuition and follow your own heart-led path. Throughout your journey with the affirmations in this book, you'll continue to develop the complex and beautiful sense of self-love that was always within you.

How to Choose Today's Self-Love Affirmation(s)

Starting your self-love journey can be intimidating. Take some of the pressure off by allowing the Universe to guide you, or take charge by listening to your inner voice. Whichever way you choose today's affirmation(s) is within your power. In this section, you'll come to understand the many possible ways to choose your daily affirmation(s).

Take a Straightforward Approach

Perhaps the most obvious way to practice your self-love affirmations is to start from the beginning of the book and work your way through it sequentially. Absorb what you can from any given day's affirmation, as it may be exactly what you need.

Lean On the Universe

Instead of reading each entry sequentially, you might choose to ask the Universe for guidance. Before you open the book, take a deep breath and ask the world to deliver the message you need to hear today. Then intuitively flip to a page. After you read the affirmation and message that the Universe has provided, reflect on how it relates to your life right now. This practice isn't restricted solely to the morning. If you feel like you need extra guidance at any time during the day, you can pick up the book and ask the Universe to lead you to the words your soul needs to hear.

Listen to Your Inner Voice

You may instead be called to choose an affirmation by listening to your inner voice today. If that's the case, you can scan through the table of contents to find an affirmation that aligns with your preferred topic. Or you may feel pulled to tune into your feelings to choose the affirmation that you need. Identifying what you need to hear the most today can be a hard process. Take a breath. Sit with what your inner voice is saying—meditate on it if you need to. Let your feelings resonate inside you, focus, and then identify the feelings. Each affirmation has its own energies and feelings; flip through the pages and see which ones align with your own.

Engage with Your Chosen Affirmation(s)

Once you choose your daily self-love affirmation(s), there are many ways you can interact with it. No single way is universally better than any other; choose the practices that feel right to you. For example, many people do affirmations in the morning, as it sets a tone for the rest of the day, but some find it more fulfilling to practice in the evening. Choosing the way that best fits you today is an act of self-love and self-care to celebrate.

Honor the Feeling of the Affirmation

As mentioned earlier, each affirmation connects with certain emotions. You may choose to interact with your self-love affirmations using your feelings first and foremost. Here's what that may look like:

If you say *I am worthy*, then take time to feel your innermost worthiness. How does it feel within your heart to know that you are wholeheartedly and undeniably worthy? In your soul? Feel the tiny tingles beneath your skin. Feel your worthiness in your breath. Feel it in every cell of your being.

Do this with every affirmation you recite.

If it's a gentler affirmation, such as *I am allowed to rest and take care of my soul's needs*, then imagine you're saying it as a parent speaking to your inner child. Feel the kindness and gentleness in the words. Allow it to feel like a deep sigh of relief within your entire body.

Some affirmations will inspire a feeling of inner power and confidence. Some will feel a little softer and quieter. Some will feel like a hug from a best friend. And all these feelings are valid. All these feelings are helpful. That said, within this book, every affirmation will always be anchored in at least one central feeling: self-love.

Read As Many Pages As You'd Like

Regardless of how you pick your first affirmation of the day, you don't have to stop at the first affirmation. You can read as many pages in one sitting as you'd like. If you feel called to read the book from cover to cover, please do. As your self-love journey deepens, your relationship with this book will likely continue to transform and evolve. Sometimes you will read one message a day, and other times you'll need to read multiple pages during one sitting.

Personalize Your Self-Love Affirmations

As you use this book, you might find it helpful to mark pages that feel especially relevant or meaningful. On index cards or sticky notes, you can write yourself little messages, such as "Read this when you're feeling sad" or "Read this when you need an extra boost of confidence." These notes will help you easily find the right words in your moments of need.

Set an Intention

As an extra step in your self-care plan, use each affirmation to help you set a daily intention. An intention is the feeling you want to embody and how you want to *be* as you move through the day. You can also think of it as the overarching mindset you want to carry throughout the next twenty-four hours.

For instance, if the affirmation is *I am deserving of true joy and happiness*, then you could set the intention to *be* the embodiment of joy in all that you do. How does it feel to move through your day with joy? What internal and external changes do you observe when you invite joy to accompany you throughout your day? What decisions do you make when you choose to prioritize your joy and make it the centerpiece of your life?

Ultimately, you should use this book to best serve your mind, body, and soul. There is no single correct approach—the only thing that matters is that it feels right to you.

You're embarking on a beautiful journey. As you move along the path of self-love, continue to return to the words on these pages and let them gently guide you back to your own inner voice and to the profound wisdom that lives inside your heart.

The Affirmations

I am **worthy** right now—just as I am—even as I continue to grow, transform, and **evolve**.

You may look at the mountain in front of you and think that if you can climb just a little bit higher—if you can *do* enough and *achieve* enough and *be* enough—you will one day reach the pinnacle of all that you are. After years of perpetual growth and self-development, you will finally reach the mountaintop and be who you always were meant to be. But that's not how it works. There is no mountain summit or ultimate marker of your growth. You're on a lifelong, never-ending journey. As you turn twenty, forty, sixty, eighty, one hundred, you will still be growing, evolving, and transforming. *You will still be blooming.* That is why it's so important to know that here, in this moment, you are worthy.

There may be aspects of yourself that you want to work on or goals you want to achieve. You may look up and see an impossibly tall mountain still in front of you. But you do not have to climb your way to the top to prove your worth. You are inherently worthy because *you are you*. This heartbeat is just as important as the next one; the breath that flows inside you is just as worthy today as it will be tomorrow. You are worthy of love and joy and success and abundance—not because you have reached the apex of your growth, but because of the extraordinary heart inside your chest that refuses to give up. So continue your journey of transformation, but know that right now, in this very moment, you are worthy just as you are. Today, with the blood and breath that flow inside you, you are enough.

I trust the **wisdom** of my inner guidance system to **lead** me in the right direction.

A force exists inside you. A soft nudge. A quiet whisper. A strange pull that can't be examined or dissected with logic and reason. It can't be easily defined or rationalized or explained. But this *thing* that you can feel deep in your core—this is your inner guidance system. It's the consciousness that exists not inside your head but deep within your heart. You might try to tell yourself that it's not real. You might try to dismiss it, suppress it, and push it away. But deep within, you know that this is as real as your blood, breath, or bones.

This feeling—this knowing—feels scary to trust, because it often leads you down unknown paths, asking you to be brave. To leap when your feet want to stay stuck to the ground. To trust what you can't see with your eyes—what you can only feel in that space that exists between breaths. But, as you begin to follow the pull, you'll start to see—*this inner force knows*. It knows what's true. It knows what's right. It knows the way. Your inner guidance system will lead you to people whose hearts match yours, to places that nurture your soul's evolution, to experiences that feel *honest* and *beautiful* and *aligned*. It will guide you down a path of true fulfillment. So don't doubt this feeling deep inside; good things happen when you trust the wisdom of your beating heart. You know so much more than you think.

I focus on what I can **control** and let go of what I cannot.

You can't control outcomes. You can't decide what someone else *does*, *thinks*, or *believes*. You can't dictate what happens in the world outside yourself. There will always be external factors that are beyond your power. But the beautiful, empowering truth that coincides with these realities is this: *It doesn't matter.* What matters is that you control your actions and daily habits.

You're in charge of how you respond to every new experience that crosses your path. You control how far you're willing to reach for the things that call to you. You write the narrative of your life—the perspective you tell it from—and whether it's a story of love and resilience or hopelessness and despair. You control whether you believe the experiences you encounter today are happening *to* you or *for* you. And, most powerfully of all, you radiate into the world the energy you want to emit. Your energy is felt. It influences how the world responds to you. If you controlled *outcomes*, you'd only be able to create a life that exists within the perimeter of what you know. But when you focus on controlling your *energy*, you call in people and experiences that exist beyond the confines of what you can even imagine. You can't control outcomes—and that's okay. Whenever you find yourself worrying about things that are beyond your control, take a deep breath and ask the Universe to guide you to your highest path and the best possible outcome. Then let it go, knowing you are being supported. Trust that the Universe has your back and that no matter what happens, the result will always be in your favor. Continually return to what you can control: your thoughts, your beliefs, and most importantly your energy.

I am grateful for my life and the **experiences** and **feelings** that have shaped me and led me to **where I am** today.

Take a step back. Survey the immensity of your life. There is the length of it, yes—the distance you've traveled and the years you've lived. This is easy to measure. But there's something else—something incalculable. Composed of the experiences and emotions that you've collected as you've reached beyond the logistical parameters of each day, this is the breadth of your life. The scope of it. It's your willingness to love, even when there aren't any guarantees that the love you give will be returned. It's the dreams you follow, never knowing if your outer world will one day match your inner vision but bravely marching forward anyway. It's the sacred sunrises, the deep exhalations, the unbridled laughter and fall-to-your-knees pain. It's the connections you build. The joy you feel. The hope you hold on to. The grief that makes a home inside your chest and never truly fades away. It's the brave, shaky steps you take on unpaved trails, walking toward that unknown place in the distance that calls to you. It's gracefully, heartbreakingly letting go of what was *meant to be* for a season but not meant to last forever.

More than that, the sum of these things is you—who you were, who you are, and who you're becoming. Continually shedding, releasing, and unraveling. Forever blooming. Letting go of pieces of yourself along the way but never losing the core of who you are: this beating heart that feels, that gives, that persists, that endures, that loves. Take a step back. Survey the immensity of your life. Inhale the gorgeous, sweeping width of it all. Exhale gratitude.

When I am struggling with a negative self-perception, I only need to look within and follow the loving guidance of my body to lead me back to self-love.

When you have a hard time loving yourself, think about your heart. Think about how on the hardest days of your life, when you weren't sure if you could keep going, it kept beating. Through loss, devastation, and grief, your heart remains steady and strong, even when the rest of you feels weak. *It never gives up on you.* And when you have a hard time loving yourself, think about your breath. Think about how effortlessly it flows to you, through you, and *for* you. In and out, in and out—a perfect, continual cycle that you can always rely on. This beautiful life-force energy chooses you every single moment. And it, too, *never gives up on you*. When you have a hard time loving yourself, think about your cells. Think about the tiniest organelles that exist within each cell, each doing its part to keep you going strong. And these microscopic components within your cells, too, *have never given up on you*.

Maybe you're having a hard time loving yourself right now, but ask yourself—can you love the microscopic structures within your body's cells that perform their functions so perfectly and indefatigably? Can you love the heart that pumps blood, which carries oxygen and gives you life? Can you see how tirelessly this system works every day because it *refuses to give up on you*? If you're having a hard time loving yourself, can you, at the very least, make a solemn vow to the smallest entity inside your body that you'll show up for it just as it shows up for you? Maybe your mind doesn't know exactly how to love yourself the way you deserve. That's okay—because your body knows. Follow its lead.

I have the **courage** to follow my heart and listen to the **voice** within.

There will be moments in your life when your heart is trying to tell you something that doesn't make sense to your logical mind. When the thoughts racing inside your head are wrapped in *hustling more* and *working harder* but your heart gently whispers, *Rest*. When your mind seeks ways it can control the outcome of the path you're on, but your heart softly says, *Surrender*. When your mind is evaluating potential paths based on what *has been*, but your heart is nudging you toward what *could be*. In these moments, your mind doubts, but your heart trusts. Your mind may see uncertainty, but your heart perceives possibilities. Sometimes your mind worries about what other people will think, but your heart knows the only thing that matters is *this feeling*. This feeling that says, *This is right* and *This is for me*. This feeling that says, *There's an unknown path ahead of me, and I must see where it leads.*

Whenever you feel that tug between your head and your heart and aren't sure which to follow, allow yourself to step away from the outside world. Take a deep breath. And ask yourself, *What does my heart want me to know, and what would it take for me to truly listen?* Write it down. Speak it out loud. Do whatever you must to make peace with your heart's subtlest messages. Because your heart knows. And some of the most important decisions of your life cannot be analyzed or reasoned or deliberated—they must be felt. Your sacred path is written inside your heart. Be brave enough to follow it.

With every decision I make and every step I take, I focus my energy on doing the bravest, most loving thing in each moment.

An honest, fulfilling, beautiful life is paved through doing the bravest, most loving thing in each moment. And this will change day by day, hour by hour—sometimes even minute by minute. Sometimes, the bravest and most loving thing you can do is to look at your to-do list, take it one line item at a time, and keep checking off boxes, knowing you'll be able to exhale deeply with relief when you're done. But other times, the bravest and most loving thing you can do is to put down the to-do list, take a step back, and take time for yourself—to sit, to breathe, to come home to yourself. And at other times the bravest and most loving thing you can do is to go all in on the pursuit of your work, your passions, your biggest goals and most heartfelt dreams.

The Universe sometimes calls for you to go all in on yourself, your healing, and on cultivating your own stillness and inner peace. Sometimes your courage reveals itself when you fight for what you love, but other times you must set your loved ones free. In some moments you must face the world unafraid by speaking loudly, and sometimes compassion requires you to let silence communicate what words can't say. When it comes to taking small steps and big leaps, when you're not sure where to go, when you *do* know where to go but you're afraid to move in that direction, ask yourself—what is the bravest, most loving thing I can do right now? Honor your answer. Move in that direction. Curate a life filled with brave and loving steps forward.

I am **brave**
enough to **try**.

This is the difficult truth about following your dreams: For life to build you up, you also must be willing to let it break your heart. You must be willing to face rejection, pain, and uncertainty. You must be willing to confront the thing you so desperately don't want to face. To stand in front of the questions that keep you up at night—*What if it doesn't work out? What if I can't do it? What if I fail?*—and not let them stop you from stepping forward. Quite simply, you must be willing to try.

If there's something that feels right, something that feels *worth it*, then you need to take a risk. Maybe it won't unfold the way you're envisioning in your mind. Maybe this experience will carry a lesson within its walls that will serve you as life gently pivots you to the next experience. And if these things happen—you'll be okay. But there's another side of this story too. The chance that it *does* work out. The chance that it's more beautiful than you can possibly imagine. The chance that there's something *honest* and *exhilarating* and *worthwhile* on the other end of this unknown path. The chance for something deeper, something truer, *something more*. Once you're willing to try, life opens for you. Anything is possible. That thing your heart is guiding you toward? You can have it. You can create it. You can experience it fully. But you must be willing to step forward and give it a chance. You must be willing to take the risk. You *must* be willing to try.

I keep my **heart** open

to every new and beautiful

thing that wants to enter my

life today.

You become so used to persevering through the hard times that they become a sort of haven—a place where you feel most comfortable. You've trained yourself to endure through what you can't control. You know how to take deep breaths and carry on through life's unexpected challenges. You've learned how to remain grateful even during your darkest days. But then something new enters your life. Something good and kind. Something that feels like a miracle. And you don't know how to accept such an incredible gift. You know how to nurture the tiniest seed of hope but don't know what to do when that intangible feeling of hope blooms into something you can touch. So you push it away.

You don't allow yourself to receive beautiful things when they land softly on your path. There may even be a part of you that feels like you aren't worthy, that you don't deserve something so precious and loving and good. But it's time you recognize this: You are so beyond worthy. You are meant for so much more than a life lived in survival mode. There is beauty and joy and bliss in this life—and it is for you. Dreams do come true. Hard work does pay off. Miracles show up when you least expect them. Joy wants to find you. Love wants to make a home inside your heart. The Universe wants to give you extraordinary things. The only thing that can ever prevent you from receiving the gifts this life has to offer is a closed heart—a false belief that you aren't worthy of them. So please, step into each day with an open heart. And when something beautiful wants to enter your life—let it in.

It's **okay** if all I do today is just breathe. I am **worthy**, regardless of what I do or don't achieve.

If today you accomplish nothing on your to-do list. If you don't make any massive, life-changing leaps. If you don't add another entry to your catalog of achievements. If you don't *hustle faster* or *work harder* or focus your energy on *doing more*. If you do nothing today but just breathe—you are still worthy. You are still enough. You are still valuable. You are still meant to be here. And you are still a gift. You still matter—regardless of what you do or don't achieve.

Rather than criticizing your need for a slowdown, give yourself extra kindness and compassion on the days when all you can do is take long breaths in and deep, soulful breaths out. And if your mind tries to convince you that taking a day off means you'll miss out or fall behind, know this: You don't manifest a beautiful and fulfilling life by working against your inner rhythm. You manifest a beautiful and fulfilling life by working *with* it—by honoring your soul's innate cycles of expansion and contraction. And even more—*and this is the secret so many of us overlook*—quite often, when you take time to pause, sink into silence, and breathe, the exact things you've been hustling for and chasing after will finally have a chance to *find you*.

I deliberately and consistently **honor** what feels right deep inside my heart and trust where my heart's **wisdom** is leading me.

Following your heart is not the easy road. It's not some idealistic, fanciful thing. No—following your heart requires extraordinary discipline. Discipline to show up every single day, even when you can't tell that anything is working out in your favor. Discipline to continue on an unpaved trail that has no mile markers, no directions, no signs pointing the way. And what can be the hardest of all: discipline to choose your own inner voice over the outer voices that may think they know best. Those outer voices can't feel that *thing* you can feel, though—that nudge deep within that says, *This is right.*

Your heart is going to take you out of your comfort zone and ask more of you than you think you can give. It's going to test you and push you to the edges of your self-perceived limits. This is not the easy road—but it's the one worth traveling. Once you start walking down your heart-led path, you will be in awe of the continual expansion of your life—the way it keeps growing and broadening and taking you to people and places and experiences you never even dreamed could exist. There will be beautiful days and hard days and everything in between—and you will fall in love with it all. With the whole journey. With every courageous step forward on the unknown path. You will fall in love with every sacred sunrise and the promise of each brand-new day. With the entirety of not just existing but *living*. And all of it—every beautiful, messy, joyous, light, heavy day ahead—it will all be worth it.

What's **meant**
for me will not
miss me.

Repeat to yourself over and over again—until the message sinks into your bloodstream and wraps around your bones and embeds itself into every breath that flows in and out of your body—*What's meant for me will not miss me.* You are not at risk of losing what's already yours. Remember that. When you feel behind. When it feels like it's taking too long. When you worry that the person or the experience or the opportunity will pass you by if you don't move fast enough. If it's meant for you, it's not going to skip past you. Just like if it *isn't* meant for you, you can't force it. But that's okay. What's coming is even more perfectly positioned and beautifully aligned.

Know that what's meant for you will arrive at the exact right time. And it isn't your responsibility to determine *when* or *how*. Your responsibility right now is to follow what the Universe and your heart are telling you. Your responsibility is to take aligned action based on what feels *real* and *honest* and *right*. Your responsibility is to release your grasp on what's no longer working to make space for something truer and more beautiful than you had ever dared to imagine. Know this deep down in your core: *What's meant for you will not miss you.* Not yesterday. Not today. Not ever.

I am worthy of being loved, **treasured**, and chosen—just as I am.

There are people in this world who will look at you like you're the most magical thing they've ever seen. They'll recognize the sacred stardust that comprises every cell of your being. They'll see beyond your physical appearance—straight into the beauty of your soul. And these people—*the right people*—will mirror your divinity back to you. In their eyes, you'll see your true self—how brilliant and stunning and utterly irreplaceable you truly are.

You are worthy and deserving of finding the people who make your soul feel at home—whose hearts fit with yours. Who show you that you are now and forever *first choice*. There are people in this world who will make sure you always know how incredibly *vital* and *needed* and *important* you are. There are people who will take your hand and hold your heart like it is the rarest, most precious gift. There are people who will choose you. There are people who will fight for you. And they'll make sure you know that you're worth choosing. You're worth fighting for. Even on the days when you have a hard time seeing it, they can see it. They can see your beauty. They can see your light. They can see *you*. Don't settle for half-hearted connections. Don't settle for relationships in which you have to shrink or contort yourself to fit someone else's vision for who they want you to be. Don't settle. *Never settle.* You are worthy of being surrounded by people who see and know all of you, and they love the person you are. They choose the person you are. They treasure the person you are—for all that you are.

I breathe unconditional **love** and **compassion** into my deepest worries and fears.

It's true what they say: Maybe if you could see all the beautiful things that await you on the path ahead, you would know there's nothing to worry about. Nothing to fear. If you knew how the Universe is orchestrating everything in your favor, you'd know only pure joy and gratitude for what's to come—for what's *already yours*. But this is also true: You are human. And all emotions are part of the human experience. All emotions are valid. All emotions are worthy of being fully acknowledged and felt—even your worries and fears. Don't suppress these feelings when they arise. Notice them with loving awareness. Hold space for them. Tend to them with kindness and compassion.

Two truths can exist at once: You can feel deep down in your core that you're on the right path, that everything will be okay, that something beautiful is unfolding—and you can still have hard moments. You can still feel the heaviness of doubt and uncertainty weighing on your shoulders. Your anxious mind can still at times cling to worry, even when your heart is gently whispering, *Trust*. Meet these uncomfortable feelings with tenderness and love. Ask the Universe to guide you back to a state of calm and peace. This is how you cultivate a beautiful world within—not by pushing difficult emotions into the darkest corners of your mind but by illuminating them with compassionate and loving light.

I am my **beautiful, authentic** self, and there's nobody else I'd rather be.

Maybe this isn't the season of *changing* yourself or *transforming* yourself or *improving* yourself. Maybe the inner work isn't about personal growth or self-development. Maybe it's not about becoming a *brand-new you*, because maybe this is the season of accepting yourself. You are you, and that's something to treasure—no one else can claim to have understood you so completely. Sometimes the inner work that needs to be done is about pouring love into every single part of you, just so you can count all the ways in which you're already enough. Maybe this season isn't about becoming something *different* or *other*, because this season is about feeling content with where and who you are. With *all that you are*.

Use this time to make peace with the parts of yourself you've been trying to run away from, because they are beautifully, authentically yours. Nurture the hidden fragments of your innermost self, telling yourself that you wouldn't rather be anyone else. Finally realize that every single part of you is already incredibly worthy, and there doesn't need to be any strings attached to your happiness. Simply understand that you've always been more than enough. Maybe this is the season when you finally end the war you've been fighting with yourself for so long. Maybe *doing the work* simply means sitting outside and watching the sky—just you and your breath and your beating heart. Not running away from yourself but not forcing anything either. Just being here, present in your body. One day, one hour, one heartbeat at a time. Deep breaths in. Full breaths out. Pouring into yourself exactly what you need.

I **sink** deeper into stillness and allow myself to move slowly through this **healing** journey, one breath at a time.

Your deepest healing will happen in the silence. Away from the self-help books and habit trackers. Away from the personal growth podcasts and health apps. Away from even friends and life coaches and mentors. There will come a time in your journey when you feel that you can do nothing at all—the bare minimum. Sitting. Breathing. Being. And it will feel strange, even wrong, at first. Like you should be trying harder. Putting in some kind of visible effort. Exerting your energy toward something that provides instant, tangible results. But this part right here—the silence, the solitude, the cocooning—this is the hardest work you will ever do. To not run or hide from yourself. To not bury yourself in busyness or reach for distractions.

To truly heal, you must simply sit in the quiet and be here with your breath. In your body. Sinking deeper into stillness. And in this space, feelings will begin to arise. Uncomfortable emotions. Things you want to run from. *Grief. Anger. Loneliness. Pain.* There is nothing to do in these moments except allow what emerges to come forward. Know that doing this work—it will take time. It won't be a single day dedicated to self-care and inner healing. This will be days, weeks, even months of feeling your way through every moment of every hour. It will not be easy. But if you can hold steady. If you can connect with your body and soul, taking it just one breath at a time. If you can allow what emerges to arise without running. Here in this space, healing will occur at the most cellular level. It is in the silence and the stillness that your deepest pain will be alchemized into love. And you will be forever transformed.

I did not come this far only to come this far. I will **keep going**. I will keep rising.

You're following your heart. You're trusting your inner wisdom. You're pouring your whole *mind* and *body* and *soul* into this beautiful, deeply felt dream. And still, there are moments. Moments when it feels like nothing is going right. Moments when you begin to doubt the vision that is painted so vividly in your mind. Moments when the life you dream about feels so far away. Sometimes there are disappointments, challenges, or delays. And (what can be the hardest to endure) long days—one after another—when it feels like nothing is happening at all.

So this is what you must do: At the end of every day, when you're tired, when you're frustrated, when you've exerted all your energy into a vision that only you can see, you have to ask yourself, *Is this still what I want?* And if at the end of each day the soft voice within still whispers *yes*, then you must continue. You must honor, trust, and protect your dream. Every single morning when you wake up, you must choose it. And you must continue to choose it, no matter how distant and untouchable it may feel. You must believe in your dream. You must guard and defend it like it is the most precious and valuable thing that exists. Because nobody else is going to make this happen for you. Only *you* can make this happen for you. And you did not come this far only to come this far. You've poured so much into this dream, and you owe it to every past and future version of you to find out what happens when you don't give up on it—when you don't give up on yourself.

I create **positive** habits that support my mind, body, and **soul**.

Daily self-care doesn't have to be big and flashy. You can create a self-care plan simply by adding small habits into your daily routine that serve your mind, body, and soul. Begin with habits that support your mental well-being: Recite affirmations, create a gratitude list, or make time for ten minutes of meditation each day. Add habits that support your physical self: Move in a way that feels good to you through activities like dance, yoga, or walking in nature. Finally, add habits that nourish your soul: Engage your creativity, allow yourself daily rest and reflection, or simply make a promise to yourself that every single evening you will dedicate an hour to offering your soul whatever it needs in that time frame.

The key to creating habits rooted in self-care is to make sure each habit feels like an offer of love to every single part of you. Habits should not feel like punishment. They should never feel like prerequisites to finally feeling worthy or good enough. And they should never be based upon how other people perceive you; maybe you think that if you can build this habit long enough, then you will be able to transform yourself into somebody who is more attractive, compelling, or valuable. No, you cannot hate yourself into self-love. The habits you create for yourself should feel like the pillars you want to build your life upon. They should be rooted in complete self-care and self-respect. Build habits—drinking more water, eating more nourishing foods, engaging in mindfulness activities—solely because you love yourself. Creating positive habits based on self-love is the only way to build tender and supportive relationships with every facet of your being.

I am so much **stronger** and more courageous than I even **realize** in this moment.

You don't always see it. Your courage. Your strength. *Your heart.* Every day, you walk this beautiful, bewildering, unknown path—this path where there are no outward signs pointing you in the right direction or maps to redirect you when you feel lost. There's just this feeling deep within that tells you that *you must keep going*—that you must see where this leads. But you don't always recognize that what you're doing is truly extraordinary. It takes immense courage to listen to your inner compass and stay true to your beating heart above all else. To value the soft, subtle whisper of your intuition over the loud, emphatic opinions of the outside world. To continue when clarity doesn't come and it feels like you're walking blindly, uncertain of the next right step. But you trust and travel through the darkness, navigating this path with only the pull of this strange, intangible feeling within to guide you. None of this is easy. It was never meant to be easy.

People often say that starting is the hardest part, but the most difficult part of traveling your heart-led path is *continuing*. Continuing to trust your heart. Continuing to walk toward the unknown. Continuing to believe and have faith and hold on to hope. Continuing day after day, month after month, year after year. Continuing is one of the bravest and most difficult things you will ever do. But you don't always see that. You're more likely to criticize yourself than recognize what a courageous and extraordinary act it is to choose the unpaved trail. Allow yourself time to step back and recognize that this road hasn't been easy—and yet, here you are. Continuing. This is the road less traveled. And you're traveling it. You are so much stronger than you have ever given yourself credit for.

I **love** myself enough to do what's **right** for me.

This is the unbreakable oath you must make to yourself—that you will love yourself enough to do what is right for you, no matter what. This is true for every single facet of your life. When you're following your dreams, you must love yourself enough to be brave. You must love yourself enough to trust your own intuition and stay true to your heart. You must continually choose to never give up in the pursuit of what calls to you. And as you walk your own chosen path, there will be days when your soul feels tired and weary. And on these days, you must love yourself enough to take time for yourself. You must give yourself permission to step away from the outside world and take deep breaths and pour into yourself exactly what you need. Because no matter what, you are always worthy of your own attention and devotion.

Love yourself enough to fight for yourself and see your own worth. When you're excited about a new idea or unexplored possibility, love yourself enough to follow the excitement. When you're torn between your head and your heart, love yourself enough to trust your inner voice. And—quite possibly the hardest but most important—when someone in your life isn't honoring you the way you deserve and the energy you give isn't being reciprocated, love yourself enough to walk away. When someone doesn't choose you, love yourself enough to choose yourself. In every single aspect of your life, that is the enduring commitment you must make to yourself—that you will love yourself enough to do what is right for you, no matter what.

I shine my **light** and allow my whole self to be seen, knowing **every** single part of me is worthy of being **loved** and embraced.

Your light is your essence. It's who you are at your core. It's the love that flows within you and the joy you feel when you're aligned with your purpose. It's everything that makes you feel excited and passionate about life. It's what makes you perfectly, uniquely you. To shine your light means to allow the entirety of you to be seen. This can be scary, because there is the chance that your light won't be received by every person you meet. But what is far scarier is spending a lifetime dimming your own light and only ever being accepted by people who want a smaller, muted, less true version of you.

When you try to hide your light out of fear of not being accepted, you end up concealing yourself from the very people who would accept you just as you are. The right people can't find you if you're hiding the parts of yourself that they would resonate with the most. Please trust that the people who are *your* people aren't even noticing the so-called flaws you see when you look at yourself. They care about whether you smiled today, if you want your favorite coffee, or if you need a hand to hold. They see you for you. They love you for you. You will never need to alter yourself to be worthy of their love and acceptance. Don't chase the approval of anyone who will only accept you if you dim your own light. You're worth more than that. Everything about you is a gift: your heart, your mind, your energy. Every cell of your being. So please—shine your light. Allow your whole self to be seen.

Every **small** step

I take today makes a

big difference.

Wherever you are in your journey, whatever you're going through right now, know that one day you're going to look back on this time, and you'll see it all so much more clearly than you do in this moment. Of course, you'll remember the life-changing decisions, the monumental wins, the steps you took that you look back upon and say, *That's when everything changed.* You'll cherish those experiences, but you'll also recognize that those big moments? They're not the ones that defined your journey. It was the tiny actions you took every single day that mattered most—the things you did that nobody ever saw. It was the unglamorous work—sometimes tedious, rarely applauded by the outside world, but so vitally essential and impactful and transformative. Sometimes, it was the research: books you read, videos you watched, notes you took. Sometimes, the connections: emails you sent, people you met, questions you asked. And oftentimes, the practice: trying something for the first time, trying something for the hundredth time, doing the exact same thing *over and over* to finally get it perfect.

Those are the moments you'll remember—the deep breaths, the small steps, the late nights and early mornings when no one was awake except for you and the moon. And at the end of it all, this is what you'll feel most grateful for. For the smallest ways you showed up for yourself. For the long hours you dedicated to your vision. For your unwavering courage and consistency and commitment. One day, you'll look back on the path you traveled and see how every tiny step you took meant something—how it all came together in ways that will still be too inexplicable to comprehend. It's these steps you're taking that make the biggest impact on your journey. It's the daily effort you exert toward your deepest dreams that you'll feel proudest of and most thankful for in retrospect.

My life **feels**, **looks**, and continually **becomes** more beautiful when I stay **true** to myself and to my heart.

Time and time again, everything comes down to three simple words: Just be you. That is the sole path to creating a beautiful, honest, fulfilling life. Be true to yourself, and listen to your intuition. Honor your beating heart. Take the path that allows you to become more of yourself. Keep following the bread crumbs that lead you back to you. If you want to know true and honest love, be you. If you want to know deep and lasting fulfillment, be you. If you want to know radiant joy, be you. If you want to live a meaningful and expansive life—*just be you*. That is your purpose here on this planet. That's your calling.

Staying true to your heart and living authentically is the sole path to a life well lived and honorably forged. This will lead you to the people you're meant to be with, to the places you're meant to go, and to the dreams you're meant to fulfill. Just be you. Just be all that you are. Just be everything that feels *real* and *honest* and *true* in your heart. Everything you're searching for begins with you. Everything you're seeking exists within you. Everything you want starts *right where you are*. Time and time again, it comes down to three simple words: Just be you. That will always lead you to where you're meant to go. That will always be the exact right path to take. That will always be more than enough.

It is never too late to **alter**

my path, follow my heart,

and **begin** again.

It really is very simple. Our time here isn't long, and it's easy to spend it in a never-ending cycle of monotony, wishing for something better. You may seek outlets to escape from an existence that doesn't fulfill your soul, or you may succumb to a comfort zone that doesn't feel comfortable at all. The chaos makes a home beneath your skin, and you become attached to the unease that embeds itself in your bones. It's very easy to believe that this way of living is normal—that every breath you take until the last is meant to be steeped in discontent. This way of living may have become normalized, but it is not normal. You aren't here just to get through this life. You are here to *live*. And no matter how deeply you're entrenched in the life you know, there is still an opportunity to alter your trajectory.

There's still time to excavate through the layers of fear and trepidation that have formed in your innermost being and dig for the truth that exists deep down in your core. Just listen to the deep-inside part of yourself that knows beyond logic or reason that *there is more* to this existence. If the breath of life still flows inside you, *there is still time*. Remember: Our time here isn't very long, and you are worthy of a life that excites your heart and fulfills your soul. Your gratitude should fill every cell of your being when you survey the immenseness and beauty of your life. You are worthy of the peace that settles into your bones when you realize you could want for nothing more than what you have right now. You are worthy of knowing genuine joy and bone-deep contentment. You are worthy of *more*. So take this chance and begin anew.

I possess beautiful **treasures** deep within me that are worth discovering and **exploring** more deeply.

Gaze upon the ocean, watch the breeze brushing against the wildflowers, look up at the night sky from the tiny corner of the earth you're inhabiting and consider the grandness of the Universe. Out there, there is something bigger than the life you know. Something *infinite*. It is beautiful and inspiring and filled with hope—and it is a direct reflection of what exists within you. The depth of the ocean mirrors the untold depths inside your very being. The beauty of the wildflowers reflects the beauty that exists within your spirit. The vastness of the Universe echoes the vastness of the world within you. And it is just as real, just as remarkable, and just as worthy of your exploration.

There is a Universe inside you filled with incredible treasures: thoughts and visions and ideas that want to be discovered. Revelations that you find only when you allow yourself the time to dig deeper. Insights that guide your unique path. Discoveries that reveal aspects of yourself you haven't yet met. Dreams of a rich and beautiful future. There is a swirl of colors that paints itself in the darkness behind your eyelids. A melody that echoes from within your soul. A story that unfolds like a movie only you can see. A design. A formulation. A creation. There is wisdom within you. There is intelligence. There is innovation. There is artistry. There is a treasure that is meant for you to find and bring forth. Inspiration begins right where you are. Ask yourself, *What is the truest thing I know right now? What do I feel? What is the truest thing I hear deep within myself?* Follow that path. Find out where it leads.

I trust that what is

meant for me

will arrive at the exact

right time.

You are a cocreator. Your task is to visualize the life you desire and take aligned action toward your most heartfelt dreams, while the Universe sets in motion the plan for how your path unfolds and when your dreams will manifest. In theory, this is straightforward. But sometimes it's hard to trust what you can't yet see. You may have hard days and heavy days and days when you're close to giving up. You may sometimes doubt whether this dream is really meant for you. The dream of success, love, or something more. But this is the unwavering truth that you need to hold on to: In a whisper of a moment—in one single but monumental breath—everything can change. All it takes is one unexpected message. One chance meeting. One look. One word. Divine timing is real, and it is always on your side. So when you're feeling discouraged, remember that you are not in this alone. You are cocreating an incredible life with the Universe, and you can trust that what is meant for you will arrive at the exact right time.

The most beautiful things often meet you unexpectedly—sometimes making a loud and bold entrance, other times drifting quietly across your path, but always perfectly aligned and divinely timed. And one day you'll look back and see how life was always guiding you to this single moment—how when you thought nothing was happening, the Universe was weaving together threads that were always meant to converge at this exact point in time. How it all came together even more beautifully than you imagined. In destined timing, your life is transformed. In an instant, the right threads are merged. At the exact right moment, something unimaginably beautiful enters your life—and it changes *everything*.

My **highest** purpose in this life is directly linked to my **authenticity**. I am everything the world needs me to be.

Purpose is hard to define. Maybe you're here to create beautiful things or make people laugh. Maybe you're here to look into another human being's tired eyes and hold their weary hands and—*for a brief but life-changing moment in time*—make them feel a little less alone. Then again, it's possible you're on this planet to lead through your own example—to walk your unique path and show others that it's okay to walk their own paths too. Maybe your purpose is just to be you.

Regardless of what your purpose is, it's linked to who you are inside: your truest, most authentic self. After all, the grandness of life exists not *out there* but *in you*—in your own unique perspective, and in the way you think, and in how you make people feel just by being every bit of your beautiful self. So maybe your purpose is to continually try to be the bravest, most loving version of yourself that you can be in each moment, or maybe it's as simple as doing the best you can every day. Every breath you take is sacred, and maybe the most important thing is to listen to the quiet pull of your beating heart. Maybe your purpose is found not in what you achieve but instead in who you are. After all, your magic was never something to be pursued; it was always waiting to be uncovered. Your journey was always meant to lead you back to yourself, because *just being you* was always more than enough.

I am **grateful** for who I was, who I am, and who I'm **becoming**.

At one time, you created a character for yourself—a version of yourself that felt safe to show the outside world. This character, you thought, would at least be accepted. Tolerated, at worst. Liked, or even—if you were lucky—loved. You held beliefs about the best and worst of yourself, trying to be who you thought everyone else wanted you to be. But in time, you began to peel back the layers—shedding, unraveling, releasing what felt disingenuous and untrue as you realized that you would rather be rejected for who you are than accepted for a false version of yourself. You learned that to become who you truly are is also to unbecome everything you are not—to extricate yourself from the fabricated identity you created to protect yourself.

While it may be tempting to dispose of your former self, the kindest thing you can do is to be gentle. Let go, but don't discard. Hold your past self with a heart full of love. For all their fear and inner turbulence, they still took the steps forward to get you here today. They made hard choices and walked a lonely, difficult path dreaming that you would become all that you are right now. As you move forward, you will build a beautiful life for your future self. But don't forget to do it for your past self too. Stay true to yourself; do it for the past self who found that impossible. Keep your heart open for the version of you who closed it in self-protection. Cultivate self-kindness for the version of you who only knew self-criticism. Honor every version of yourself that you've ever been. The person you were, the person you are, and the person you're becoming are all worthy of your unwavering love.

When I'm **feeling** overwhelmed, I allow myself the time and space to **pause**, step back, and breathe.

At times when you can't imagine taking a break, you must. When tension is growing heavier and heavier in your head until you can no longer navigate through the density of your own thoughts, pause. Pause when you know that it would take just *one more thing*—one more task, one more criticism, one more problem—for you to fall apart. When you can sense that you are on the cusp of something irrevocable. That is when you must remove yourself from it all. Physically, if you can. Mentally, if that is your only option. Whatever you can do, whatever it takes—you must allow yourself this time. Ten minutes. Five minutes. A short walk around the block. This is not the time to come up with a plan of action for the future or to think about the past. Nothing is allowed during this time except for the present moment. *Deep breaths in. Full breaths out.*

What are five things you can see in the world around you? What are five things you can hear? Touch? Smell? Play the simplest games with your external world. Name everything in your current environment that is red. Green. Blue. Yellow. Place your hand on your chest. Feel the steady beating of your heart. Repeat grounding affirmations. Do one kind thing for your mind, body, or soul. *Deep breaths in. Full breaths out.* This is what you must do when the stress feels too heavy to hold. You must put your own well-being first. The *stuff* will still be there when you return: the work, the people, the to-do lists. But your mind will feel calmer. Your focus will be sharper. Your energy will be restored. When you think you don't have time for it is exactly when you need it the most. *And you will be better for it.*

I am **allowed** to

put myself first, and I am

empowered

to say no to anything that

doesn't feel right to me.

You're allowed to say no to whatever doesn't support your well-being or serve your highest good. Say no if it's going to hurt you or the energy just feels *wrong*. There are moments when your time isn't being valued, your needs aren't being considered, or something goes against what you believe in. If it simply feels like a *no* within your body, even if you can't explain why. If the *yes* that lingers at the tip of your tongue is only due to a compulsion to people-please. In all these scenarios, your *no* is valid, important, and essential.

To say no to what doesn't support your well-being is to say yes to yourself. You may disappoint others by not being everything they *want* you to be. But you must not disappoint yourself or let yourself down for someone else's sake. This doesn't mean that you're selfish or uncaring. It doesn't mean that you don't make compromises—that you don't sacrifice for the people you love. And it doesn't mean that you only do the things that you *want* to do; there will always be circumstances in which you must choose a less attractive option that you know in your heart is right. But you must set boundaries and honor what you feel deep within. *No* can also be born out of love—love that you are worthy of giving to yourself as freely as you give to others. You are allowed to choose yourself when you need rest, something doesn't feel right, or it feels like no one else is looking out for your needs. Above all else, you must be the guardian of your own mind, body, and soul. Just remember: The people who truly love, care for, and respect you will ultimately want you to choose you too.

I am replacing worry with **peace**, self-doubt with **self-trust**, and self-criticism with **self-compassion.**

You replace worry with peace by becoming aware of your thoughts. Step back and allow yourself to become a nonjudgmental observer of your own mind. Notice what you're thinking about. *I'm thinking about what might go wrong, what the repercussions of that are, and how others will view me.* Acknowledge the worry: Is it serving you? If not, remind yourself that the worry exists to protect you, but that you don't need it now—that you can let it go. Take a deep, full breath through the nose. Inhale peace. Exhale the heaviness.

You replace self-doubt with self-trust by imagining that there exists a timeline in which a future version of yourself has already lived through today. They know the outcome of every decision and know where this journey leads. Then you imagine the supportive hand of your future self, guiding you down this path. They're the reason you possess this unexplainable knowing deep within your heart. They gave you the nudge to move forward. And you realize that you can trust your future self's guidance; *they will not let you down*.

You replace self-criticism with self-compassion by viewing yourself through the eyes of love. You acknowledge your perceived flaws, failures, and mistakes. And then you ask, *What would the voice of love say to each of these parts of me?* If the inner critic is still being relentlessly cruel, think about your best friend. What if they were saying these self-deprecating things? What would you say to them to help them silence their inner critic? Take the message you would offer to your best friend in their darkest moments, and say it to yourself. Above all, that is what you must always strive for through your journey—to continually treat yourself like you are your own best friend.

I trust and **believe** in my enduring courage, strength, and **resilience** to always carry me through difficult situations.

What if something *does* go wrong? What if there are unknown challenges awaiting on the path ahead? What if the known challenges materialize just as you had feared? And what if, still, you know with every cell of your being that no matter what happens, you'll be okay? Maybe you start to make the big speech and forget your words, or you submit the application and receive a rejection letter. You may stumble, fall, or be turned away. Nothing may go to plan.

You may believe that your power lies in your ability to think positively—that the way to overcome your deepest fears is by convincing yourself that nothing bad will ever happen. But your real power is in your self-trust. When you can stand *tall* and look fear straight in the eyes—when you can allow yourself to truly *see* your fears—you are powerful. See the thing that's stopping you from moving forward. Visualize the worst-case scenario playing out in your mind's eye. Then visualize what happens afterward. You stumble, but you recover. You persevere. You carry on. And through this journey, something *truer* and *more beautiful* arises. The denial leads to a divine redirection. The heartache leads you on a sacred journey of self-love. The one closed door reveals a hundred open ones. Something extraordinary emerges because you trusted that, no matter what, you'd be okay. Sometimes, the worst-case scenario does happen. There are obstacles, rejections, and dismissals. There is a bumpy, imperfect road ahead. You may wish you had the foresight to know what awaits you, but it's far more important that you know this: Your heart has never failed you. You are resilient and brave and so incredibly strong. And no matter the outcome of taking these next steps—you're going to be okay.

I allow myself to dream **bigger** than I ever have before and leave room for things to turn out even **better** than I can imagine.

One day, you're going to realize it was never out of reach. The dream you thought was maybe *a little too big*. The goal you worried you set *a little too high*. The vision of a beautiful life filled with *joy* and *love* and *fulfillment*. And even more: You'll realize that you were dreaming too small. That you're capable of *so much more* than you could ever imagine. That every big dream you've ever had is *just the beginning* of what's possible for you. Because the Universe isn't limited, and you're not either. What you're dreaming about and envisioning when you close your eyes—that's just the starting point. The Universe is vast and limitless and infinite. *And so are you.*

Allow yourself to question the limits you've imposed upon your own imagination. What if you dreamed beyond the confines of your physical reality? What if you replaced what seems *reasonable* with what feels *true*? What if instead of trying to convince yourself to accept less, you asked the Universe to lead you to more? Allow yourself to dream with the knowledge that what you're dreaming about is only a tiny glimpse into what's possible. Embrace the idea that there is something so much deeper, richer, and more expansive out there for you. And then give yourself permission to take small steps toward your dreams—with the belief that things will turn out even better than you can imagine. There's no such thing as dreaming too big. If the vision exists within you, it can be created outside of you. Have the courage to expand your aspirations and reach farther than you have ever before. Then leave room for something even truer and more beautiful than you had envisioned to emerge.

I find deep inner peace when I **trust** that the Universe always provides me with exactly what I **need** at the exact right time.

Peace is cultivated through knowing that everything is always working in your favor. It's built by trusting that the Universe is on your side—that you're never truly alone. It's found in remembering that you can't lose what's meant for you, and if a person or an experience is meant to stay, it will stay. Peace is strengthened through surrender. It's unearthed from within when you allow yourself time to sit in stillness, feel your heart gently beating inside your chest, and exhale. It's built layer by layer as you talk to the Universe and hand over your worries to something bigger than yourself.

Peace is found through relinquishing control. It's knowing that you can't control people. You can't control whether someone or something is meant to remain in your life forever. You can't control the world outside of you. But you can build a world within that feels safe and loving and secure. You can know with every cell of your being that what's meant for you will not miss you. You can trust that what chooses to leave is making space for something even more perfectly matched and beautifully aligned. Peace is embedded in your roots when you realize that you are eternally loved, supported, and protected. It makes a home inside you when you trust that every step of your journey reveals itself at the exact right time. It permeates every breath you take when you view your life through a lens of gratitude and appreciation. Peace is built and strengthened through faith: faith in the Universe, faith in your own steady heart, faith in what you can't always see or touch but can feel—what you know to be true deep inside yourself.

My **commitment** and **dedication** to my goals is paying off in ways I can't yet see.

Everything may change for you overnight; the vision you've been imagining for so long becomes something you can see, something you can hear, something you can touch. A new world reveals itself to you in an instant. And it may feel like it all happened so quickly. To outsiders, it will appear as if it drifted so effortlessly onto your path. But there are layers beneath the visible world that only you can see. Only you know the foundation upon which the life you've created was formed. Hours of building, practicing, struggling, and healing. Hours of transforming. Hours of doing, being, unraveling, releasing, and becoming. Hours of surrendering, trusting, allowing, and believing. You spent so much time living in the darkness of your own mind, questioning yourself, hearing the whispers of your deepest fears telling you that you're not worthy, that you're not enough, that this dream isn't meant for someone like you. And you pushed past those voices, refusing to give up on yourself.

All that time, you were *fighting for this*. So, yes, your achievement happens quickly on the surface. Success blooms overnight, but nobody else sees the thousands of big and small steps you took to reach what was once just a dream that you couldn't let go of. Your world changes in an instant, but that instant was formed by the hard choices you made, the struggles you overcame, the fears you didn't run from, and the energy you poured into building a beautiful life. Some people may see it simply as good luck, but the truth is much more profound: Your life transformed because you didn't give up on your dream and it didn't give up on you.

I know that **healing** is not a linear journey, and I **accept** my good days and bad days as they come.

Allow yourself to feel every emotion that arises—even the ones that hurt. *Especially the ones that hurt.* Do this for yourself, because the only way out is through. To grow and move forward, you must feel what you need to feel while pouring endless love and compassion into yourself with every hard-earned breath you take. This is especially true when an old wound from your past reopens—when something you thought you had healed from reemerges as if the pain is still raw and brand-new. This can be brought on by the smallest reminder or trigger. Something you see or hear. An experience in your outer world that causes a storm to take over your inner one. And you may think something is wrong with you for feeling this way. A thousand *should*s may swirl through your mind. You *should* be over this and be able to push past it. You *should* be stronger than you feel right now. But those *should*s are lies.

You are not broken or weak. Nothing is wrong with you. This is part of the hard, imperfect, nonlinear journey of healing. This is what it means to be a human who knows that love, heartache, and grief are often inextricably intertwined. And there's no timeline or rule book for healing. So please—be gentle with yourself. Care for yourself the way you would for someone you love. Acknowledge the courage and strength it takes to keep your heart open, to remain soft, to feel these heavy and difficult emotions without running. Even if you don't feel so strong right now. Even if all you can manage to do today is hold yourself together. One day, you'll reflect and see that this experience isn't proof of your weakness but of your incredible, unyielding strength.

I choose to **create** a **life** that feels good to me from the inside.

You walk into a dressing room and try on clothing. You look in the mirror and observe how each piece looks on your body. The mirror doesn't tell the full story, though. The outfit may look perfect. The salesperson may claim that it was made for you. But there's a sense of discomfort within—it may look good, and it may be praised by strangers, but it doesn't *feel* right. It doesn't feel like *you*. And that is the highest standard you must set for the smallest and biggest choices you make in your life: *Does it bring me closer to myself or pull me farther away?* This is true for the clothing you wear and the hairstyles you choose, and on a larger scale it's true for the paths in life you decide to follow. It is never about what other people will think.

Whether you travel the world, raise a family in the suburbs, go back to school, or focus on your career, it's your life and it should feel good to you. Your life does not have to look like anyone's but your own. What is most important, above all else, is that it feels honest. That it feels right. *That it feels like it's bringing you closer to yourself.* This doesn't mean you don't value the insight that others can provide, but the people whose opinions you should value most are those who also want you to feel more like you. Remember: Your life is your canvas. The shapes and colors you paint on it are entirely yours to choose. Outsiders may not understand what you're creating—it doesn't matter. It doesn't matter how your canvas—*how your life*—looks from the outside. It only matters how it makes you feel from the inside.

Any **progress** I make, no matter how small, is still progress in the **right** direction.

You tell yourself that you should be doing more or be better. That what you're doing is *never enough*. Self-criticism is easy. Maybe it's second nature. Maybe you constantly search for your own inadequacies and are harder on yourself than anyone else could ever be. You are your own harshest critic. This is a never-ending spiral: to continually tell yourself that *it is never enough*, no matter how far you go and how much you accomplish. Never-ending, unless you consciously choose to end it. Unless you begin to ask yourself, *Am I doing the best I can?* Because that is the only measurement you need to use to evaluate the steps you're taking. If you take the tiniest step forward today, but you pour every single bit of time and energy you have into that step, then it is enough. If you practice something for hours and don't feel like you've gotten any better in that time, but you learn what *not* to do for next time, that is enough. If you do the best you can with the knowledge and skills you possess in this moment, while aiming to continually improve, that is enough.

Don't measure your progress based on what others are doing or how far along they are on their own journeys. The only thing that matters is that you did the best *you can* today. You took a tiny step forward. You put your energy into the things that mattered. *You moved in the right direction.* Promise yourself every morning that you will do the best you can. When you lie in bed at night, make another unbreakable oath that you will show up for yourself again tomorrow. Keep doing the best you can with the time, energy, knowledge, and skills you have. That is the true measurement of success.

I trust that I **possess** everything I need inside me to walk through every season of my life with **strength** and **grace.**

When you don't know what to trust, trust your track record. You have survived the hardest days of your life, through the darkest nights and coldest winters. Even when it felt like your life was falling apart, you held on to that last ember of hope inside you. And that single ember can outlast even the most raging of storms—it's inextinguishable. *Trust that it will continue to burn.* When you don't know what to trust, trust your inner strength. You have lived through experiences that only you know about and felt pain that you would never wish upon another soul. Trust that there is something stronger and more powerful than you even realize. And if the time comes when you must tap into your inner strength, trust that you will.

When you don't know what to trust, trust your heart. Trust that it has remained steady and unwavering through every hard, heavy, impossible day of your life. Trust that when you feel like you have no fight left, your heart will carry you. And even if the rest of your body wants to give up, your heart won't. It will continue to battle. *It will never abandon you.* When you don't know what to trust, trust your courage. When you must face the thing that scares you, trust that you will summon your bravery and look fear in the eyes, and you won't back down. Trust that you are a force that cannot be undone by fear—that something inside you is far more powerful than fear. *Trust that you will not be defeated.* When you don't know what to trust, trust yourself. Trust your resilience and ingenuity. Trust that you're going to be okay, and that no matter what happens, you will always rise.

I notice my **thoughts** and feelings without judgment and release any **energy** that does not serve my mind, body, or soul.

Begin to consciously notice what's happening inside you by, first, removing yourself from your work and to-do lists. Find somewhere you can be alone: your bedroom, garden, or kitchen floor. Sit and take a deep breath and another—as many deep breaths as you need. Then place a hand on your heart. Inhale. Feel the soft thumping beneath your fingertips. Let this become your entire world—the gentle tapping of your beating heart. Exhale. As you repeat this process, your mind inevitably starts to wander. You think about a comment someone made at work this morning and an errand you need to run tonight. You realize you've gotten so lost in your thoughts that you've forgotten where you even are. So gently allow yourself to release these thoughts and return to your heart center.

This cycle repeats: You breathe, you feel, you think, you notice, and you return to your heart center. You stay here for a while, in this quiet space, until it's time to return to the outside world. Then you get up and continue with your day. Maybe you feel a little better. Maybe not. But still, you come back to this space tomorrow. And the next day. And the next. And slowly, something within you shifts. You become a conscious observer of your thoughts more and more throughout your day. You can return to your heart center even when you're surrounded by outside noise. You begin to feel more in control of your energy. You recognize your own innate power to choose the thoughts and feelings that serve your well-being and let go of the rest. This sense of peace and stability becomes embedded in your core. The world around you may not look any different, but suddenly everything has changed. You have changed. In the stillness, you have transformed.

I choose to **trust** my heart-led **path**, even when it doesn't make sense to others.

There will be a moment in your life when your heart will nudge you toward an unknown path and ask you to trust in something that you can feel but not see. Something that feels like a bigger risk than you have ever taken before. Maybe you'll have to choose between traveling the familiar road that your mind deems *safe* or veering toward the unpaved trail that is *right*. Then you must determine the greater risk: choosing the untraveled path or *not* choosing it. You'll have to decide whether you're ready to trust your heart above all else. You may have to do something that nobody will be able to fully understand but you. Some people may support you; some people may not. But nobody else will be able to see your vision or feel what you feel. And you will have to be okay with that. You'll have to be willing to trust your feelings and visions, even if you must walk alone for a while. Throughout life, your heart will ask you to have faith in your own innate wisdom: *Go here*, your inner voice will whisper. *This is the way.*

There will be a moment when this feeling, this knowing, this whisper will feel like the only real thing that exists. And you will no longer be able to ignore it. You will no longer be able to live a life that feels like it is somebody else's. You will no longer be able to take another step toward anything that doesn't feel genuine and authentic to you. And the moment you choose to say yes to honoring your heart above all else—when you decide you cannot deny what feels *right* and *honest* and *true* for a second longer—that's when your life can truly begin.

Every emotion that arises during my self-love journey is valid. I compassionately allow myself to feel these emotions without judgment or criticism.

Your self-love journey is full of many emotional highs and lows. When the anger comes, you'll know you're on the right path. At first, you may feel anger toward people in your past who treated you poorly. You'll recognize when your kindness was taken for granted or taken advantage of—when you continually gave without receiving anything in return. This anger will simmer for a while. But then there will be another deeper layer. You'll turn your anger on yourself. You'll become angry that for so long you couldn't see your worth. That you settled for less than you deserved. That you spent so much energy trying to be the person others wanted you to be instead of embracing your authenticity. You'll become angry for all the ways you tried to reshape yourself to receive acceptance from others. That you betrayed yourself in the pursuit of external love. That you accepted half-hearted attention when you're worth wholehearted devotion. You'll be angry that you couldn't see yourself clearly.

When the anger comes, don't push it away. Allow yourself to feel it. Understand what it's telling you. You're angry because you're finally recognizing your own worth. You're angry because you can no longer imagine trying to change yourself to receive another person's love or acceptance. You're angry because *you will never abandon yourself again*. When you feel this anger, that's when you know something has permanently shifted inside you. You've been through a transformative journey. You're finally accepting the love you were always worthy of receiving. So when the anger comes, feel it all. Thank it for what it's showing you. And then, with love and gratitude in your heart, allow it to be released.

I may not be fearless, but I am **brave**. I have the courage to **always** do what is right for me.

Fear is a dragon in the distance. It cannot be vanquished in your mind. You can affirm your bravery. You can remind yourself that your courage runs deeper than your fear. You can analyze and gently probe the root of your fear. But no matter how many circles you run around it, the dragon itself doesn't disappear. No—to win the battle with fear, you must take the most straightforward and least nuanced approach. You must march straight into the fear. There are no shortcuts. No alternative routes.

The life you've been dreaming about, the thing you care most about—it's all on the other side of the dragon. Everything you want is *right there*. And it may feel impossible to move forward. The anticipation of what you'll see when you look the dragon in the eyes might threaten to stop you before you can even get close to it. But this is what you need to remember when you know that you cannot wait a second longer—when it's time to finally face the thing that's been haunting your mind. The dragon in the distance has an enormous shadow that looms over the landscape. *But that shadow is an illusion.* As you get closer to the dragon, you'll realize that it's actually quite small. That you are undoubtedly much bigger. That there is nothing it can do to stop you from walking straight past it. And *that* is the essence of fear: It is made so much bigger in your mind. The dragon may always exist. It may always be a character in your story, walking beside you along your sacred journey. That's okay. You don't need to be fearless. You just need to remember that you are bigger than the dragon—and it cannot stop you from moving forward.

I control my own **energy**.

I'm the only one who chooses

how I **feel** in each moment.

One of the most important boundaries you set is the one nobody else will ever see. It is the bubble that you create around yourself—an invisible force field. All day, every day, outside energy will try to enter your bubble. It comes from the people you interact with, the content you consume, and what you see and hear in the world around you. Energy is everywhere. But only you get to decide what gets to come in and what goes out of your bubble. Only you control your energy, and only you get to choose how you feel in each moment. You may forget this power sometimes. Outside energy—other people's anger, anxieties, and fears—enters without your conscious awareness. Their energy becomes so prevalent that it begins to overpower your own.

So this is what you must do: You must be willing to observe your thoughts, emotions, and energies. *What am I thinking? How am I feeling right now? Does this feel like it belongs to me?* And then ask: *Do I want to continue to carry this?* You are not required to carry other people's energy. You might choose and even want to—when a friend comes to you with their grief, you may share the weight of their pain so they don't have to carry it alone. You may also welcome the feeling of getting to share in another's joy, triumph, and celebration. What's important is knowing that *it is always your choice*. Even if the energy that circulates around you is filled with tension and unease, you can lock it out. You can choose to remain calm and steady. You can choose to offer a sense of safety and stability to the people around you. You can choose to radiate peace.

As I continue to show up for my **future** self, I'm also able to step back and appreciate the path I've **traveled** and how far I've come.

Do it for your future self. This is a valuable mindset to maintain as you push yourself to do all those tedious and unpleasant things you don't really want to do. Waking up early. Running errands. Initiating hard conversations. Pushing yourself in uncomfortable ways. Your future needs you. Your future self is shaped by you. Many of their life circumstances are determined by the things you do today. And the hope is that your future self will be able to reflect on all the incredible progress they've made and recognize how far they've come. And when they look around at the life they're living, they'll think back on the things you're doing today. And all they'll feel is immense gratitude to you—for the way you're showing up, and for your consistency and endurance.

At some point, though, it's important to recognize that in this moment you *are* a version of your future self. You're the person you were dreaming about ten years, five years, even just a year ago. And even if all you can see are more mountains in the distance, allow yourself to take a moment to turn around and look back upon all the mountains you've already climbed. What hard things have you had to do to get to where you're standing today? How does your life look different than it did before? What were the small steps you took consistently, deliberately, and without fail? Right now, you are a version of your future self. You're the person you once dreamed of being. You may not yet be exactly where you want to be, but take a moment to reflect upon the path you've traveled. Remember what it took to get here. Sink deeper into appreciation for this moment you're living in right now.

I love myself **fully**, even the parts I once judged and neglected, because every part of me is **worthy** of my love, care, and attention.

Your love is your light. When you focus on parts of yourself to nurture and appreciate, you shine a soft beam of light onto them. When you tend to your soul's deepest needs or joyfully explore your mind's boundless imagination, these aspects of yourself shimmer in the light of your love. But there are parts of your innermost self that don't receive that light. Maybe you're deeply competitive and prone to anger when you lose, or you're resentful when others succeed—especially when they get something *you* want. Maybe you try to manipulate others into giving you their attention. Maybe the light doesn't reach your bossiness, moodiness, or defensiveness, or how your mind is always searching for *something* to be negative about. These are the shadows that exist within you—the aspects of yourself that you've deemed unacceptable. It's not that you ignore these parts of yourself; you know them all too well. But you label them as *wrong* and push them away. However, the pushing doesn't push them farther away; it pushes them deeper within, where they gain greater power over you.

You can never fully escape your own darkness—and that's okay, because it's not something you need to escape from. When you notice an aspect of yourself that you want to push into the darkest corners of your being, take a moment to pause. Summon your courage. And allow yourself to walk into the darkness, bringing with you the light of your love. You don't need to indulge your feelings; simply acknowledge them. View them with honesty. Compassionately accept their existence within you, and simply listen. Allow your darkness to be fully illuminated by your love. By doing this, you're not giving power to your shadows. You're giving power to your light.

I am **grateful** for all that I have in this present moment, and I am **excited** to create an even more **vibrant** and beautiful future.

Gratitude and desire are not mutually exclusive. Genuine thankfulness for the experiences you're having doesn't mean there are no new dreams to be unearthed from within. Reaching for those dreams doesn't mean you don't appreciate all the beautiful and mysterious ways your path has unfolded, shaping you into the person you are today. Gratitude and desire are not a tug-of-war between *what is* and *what could be*. They are not two separate entities, one standing on each of your shoulders, one labeled *good* and the other *bad*. No. Gratitude and desire are allies, united in their purpose to help you create a gorgeous and expansive life.

Gratitude keeps your feet anchored to the earth, while desire draws your eyes up toward the sky. Gratitude is the gateway to your daily miracles. It reminds you that there is a life to be lived right here in this moment—that when you take the time to pause and notice, this life you're living is remarkable. It helps you to cherish the people and experiences that bring love and joy and meaning to your world. It is the foundation on which an extraordinary life is built. Meanwhile, desire reminds you to never stop looking up at the stars. It's a nudge to follow your curiosity. To step beyond the perimeter of your comfort zone. To discover what experiences exist beyond the confines of what you know. And with gratitude as your anchor, it's safe to explore. Because no matter how far you wander, gratitude will always bring you back to the breath that's flowing through you right now. So know that you can continue to appreciate while also continuing to dream. Both are essential elements for creating a full and beautiful life.

My **personal** journey is about not just what I achieve externally but who I **become** along the way. I embrace each experience as an opportunity to grow, **transform**, and learn more about myself.

Imagine there's a timeline in front of you. On this timeline, you mark this moment right now with a single black dot. Farther down on the timeline, you draw another black dot. This one represents the moment when it happens—the dream or goal is realized. The vision that's been etched in your mind becomes real. These black dots aren't the beginning or the end of your story, but they're important moments. They matter not just because of what you've achieved externally but because of *who you are* in each moment. You will not be the same person, when you reach that second black dot, as you were at the first. The long expanse of space between is your journey—the journey you are meant to go on. You'll uncover different aspects of yourself on this path: your bravery, resilience, strength, determination, and grit. You'll travel through the dark forests where you face your deepest fears. You'll find yourself exploring, curiously questioning, and learning or unlearning. And you'll walk into your hardest battles—sometimes with external forces but mostly with your own inner demons.

This journey will provide you with lessons and experiences that you never would have had otherwise. That is why the dream exists within you—not just because of what you gain and achieve externally by fulfilling your heart's deepest desires, but because of who you become along the way. One day, you will look at the timeline of your life and realize that the black dots are not the story. The story is the person you became in the spaces between. The story is the journey you took to become who you were always meant to be.

How someone else **treats** me is not a reflection of my worth. I am **worthy**, regardless of what somebody else does or says.

There are apologies you'll never get and words you deserve to hear that will never come. There are conversations you'll never have. Questions that will never be answered. There are quick explanations that, if only they'd offer, could save you from spending years believing you did something wrong. And you could replay events in your mind over and over forever, wondering if something was your fault. Thinking about all the ways you could've changed the outcome. Obsessing over how you could've saved what was lost. But you need to know: It wasn't you. It was never you. How they treated you was never a reflection of your worth. You are worth so much more than how they made you feel. You're worth the peace you cultivate from letting go of what no longer serves you. You're worth the love that blooms within you as you reconnect with your innermost self. Each moment of joy you rediscover and the fulfillment you find from people and places and experiences that nourish your soul—that know how to hold your heart the way it deserves to be held—all reflect how much value you have. You're worth soft sunrises and the promise of new beginnings. You're worth being enchanted by life again. Don't let anyone cause you to harden your heart or close yourself off from the magic of living. They don't deserve that much power. And your soft heart is worth protecting, cherishing, and holding on to.

As I fall deeper in love

with myself, the outside

world becomes a reflection

of the radiant

world within me.

This is the secret: It all begins with loving yourself completely. The dreams coming true. The life of joy, magic, and fulfillment. The soul-level connections with people who think your smile is the best part of their day. Everything you seek begins with self-love—with learning how to hold your own heart like it's the most precious and valuable gift. With building a home inside yourself that feels safe and warm and secure—a place where you can take off your armor and sink deeper into your own being and feel held by the soft light of the Universe. It begins with seeing yourself the way *love* sees you—like the breathtakingly exquisite vision you are. The life you're dreaming about doesn't begin when you're able to convince other people that you're worthy. It won't reveal itself to you when you finally reach some elusive state of perfection. It begins with the love you accept from your own precious heart. It begins with the deep-rooted knowing that you've always been worthy of love—from others, from the Universe, and most importantly from yourself.

What you're looking for isn't *out there*. It's right here. It's in the darkest corners of your own inner being. It's in the places that need your love the most. Everything you've been searching for is already inside you. Everything you've been chasing is already yours. Love begins *right where you are*. The love you pour into yourself will seep into every aspect of your life and expand in ways you can't even imagine. Soon, you'll see—when you fall in love with yourself, the world falls in love with you back. The outside world mirrors the radiant world you've created within.

I listen to my body's **wisdom** when it asks me to contract my energy and **honor** my softer, slower seasons of life.

If you aren't feeling it, you can't force it. You can't force your energy to expand when it is begging to contract. You can't force yourself to push forward when your spirit is asking you to pull back. You can't force life to move at your pace. There's only one thing you can do when your energy is asking you to slow down: *Trust*. Trust what your energy is telling you. Trust that maybe this chapter of your life isn't meant for *hustling* or *grinding* or *achieving*. Maybe this isn't the part of the story where you scale mountains or collect gold medals or build empires. Maybe the era of constant effort and exertion is meant to be put on pause for just a little while. And maybe all you need to do right now is keep trying to create beautiful things and build meaningful relationships and walk toward the things that feel real and honest and right.

So follow your joy and search for life's hidden magic and reconnect with your inner child's sense of curiosity and wonder, or sit in silence and take slow, deep breaths and listen to the soft whispers of your beating heart. Spend your evenings watching the sky as you talk to the Universe and trust in a plan that you can't yet see. Because maybe somewhere in the quiet, in the stillness, there's a path that will lead you to somewhere more beautiful than you can imagine. And you simply need to become more of yourself, to let your heart guide you back to you, to access your wildest dreams. All you need to do right now is build a soft, safe space within your own being. Right now, surrender, allow, and trust. Let that be enough.

I am eternally connected to the **divine** source of the Universe. It is always speaking to me through **signs**, symbols, messages, dreams, and my own innate intuition.

The Universe has so many ways to shine its divine guidance upon you. Speak to the earth, the trees, the ocean. Speak to the moon. Speak to the stars. Speak to life itself. Speak aloud your worries and fears. And then speak your dreams, gratitude, and desires. Every thought and feeling that's buried deep inside you, everything that's weighing heavily on your mind—speak it out loud. At every moment, you are closely connected to a divine force that is so much bigger than yourself. Be open and courageous enough to communicate with the Universe like it's your most trusted and devoted companion. Express when you're sad, lost, or lonely. Declare when you're *unmotivated*, or when you *want to make a change* but don't know where to start. Say when you *don't know what to do*, or when you're *not sure what your purpose is* anymore. Ask for the Universe to show you a miracle. Ask it to reveal what you need to know. Ask for clarity, guidance, or a sign. Ask—and *listen*.

After you ask, notice how the Universe is speaking back to you. Notice the symbols that appear in your outer world. Notice the strange, unexplainable coincidences that occur when you're least expecting them. Notice the messages that keep repeating over and over. And as you sink deeper into the quietness of the earth and immerse yourself in silence, notice how life speaks to you from within. You are eternally connected to the Universe through your own inner knowing and your heart's wisdom. Through thoughts, ideas, and feelings. Through a soft voice inside you that feels honest and loving and pure. Unburden yourself to the sky. Commune with the mountains. Visit with the life-force energy that flows within and all around you. Speak—and *listen*. The Universe is speaking back.

I honor the **promises** and **commitments** I make to myself.

Make these tiny, sacred promises to yourself: Promise that you will never give up on yourself or your dreams. Promise that you will continue doing things that excite you and make you feel incredibly grateful to be alive. Promise that you will move courageously toward your heart's truest visions for the future. Swear to walk through every open door of opportunity with faith, courage, and belief. Vow to walk away from situations that don't serve your growth, help you to heal, lift you up, or support your total well-being. Promise to feed your mind, body, and spirit with love and devotion every day. Vow to speak to yourself with gentleness and compassion in the privacy of your own mind. Swear to nurture your shadows just as tenderly as you nurture your light. And promise that you will continue to seek miracles and wonder in this Universe. You will continue to be exactly the person you were created to be. You will continue to be the light the world so desperately needs.

When you make yourself a promise and keep it, you're showing yourself respect. Every time you honor a commitment you make to yourself, your self-love blooms and your sense of self-worth deepens. You can choose a different vow to make to yourself each morning. You might start with, *No matter what happens today, I promise to remember my worth.* Then, through every encounter and experience, whisper your self-promise like it is an everlasting oath. This is not only how you show yourself loyalty but also how you teach yourself how you deserve to be loved—by honoring your commitments, no matter what. So make tiny, sacred promises to yourself. Write them down. Carry them with you. Grip them tightly. Don't let go. Make them unbreakable.

I choose **myself**. I choose my dreams. I choose to honor what feels **right** to me.

There's this vision you can't get out of your mind—this beautiful dream that at times feels so close and still so far away. And you might ask yourself what you need to do to create this vision in your outer world. There is one and only one thing: You *must* choose yourself, your dreams, and your sense of what's right. Consistently. Deliberately. Even if it means letting go of what you once thought you could not live without. When an experience or opportunity comes that doesn't feel right deep down in your core, you must be willing to walk away. When something feels off about your current path, you must trust that your intuition knows something that your cognizant mind can't quite comprehend. When it feels tempting to mold yourself into a more agreeable shape to receive love and acceptance from another, you must close your eyes and take a deep breath and decide that *no*—no, you're going to choose *you* this time. You're going to choose your incredible, worthy, authentic self and the dreams and morals within you. You must let go of what your mind *thinks* you want in order to receive what your soul actually needs. Choosing yourself requires trust in what you can't see but can *feel* deep inside yourself. It means honoring your own inner wisdom—trusting that the directions to that beautiful vision exist inside you. Looking within to uncover the map, the compass, and the key. When you choose yourself, you send an energetic message into the Universe that says you are worthy of being chosen. It shows that you respect yourself, your values, and your beliefs. It's a path paved in authenticity, allowing you to offer the most open and honest version of yourself to the world. Choose yourself, and you'll find that the world will choose you too.

When my **dream** comes true and something **beautiful** wants to enter my life, I allow myself to **receive** it, knowing that I am always worthy.

When something beautiful wants to enter your life, know that you are worthy of it. Your first instinct may be to deny what's meant for you because of fear. Fear that this dream or opportunity isn't real. Fear that it's too good to be true. Fear that it'll all go away as quickly as it came. But please—don't turn it away. Don't reject your divine destiny because of vicious and self-sabotaging thoughts circling through your mind that say you shouldn't have something this good. That these kinds of things only happen to other people. That you're *too much*. That you're *not enough*. That you aren't worth such a precious gift. Sometimes a good thing is just a good thing. Sometimes it *is* real. Sometimes it doesn't stay with you for a single breath, for a single chapter—sometimes it's yours for the whole entire book. And sometimes beautiful things can adorn your path without ugly shadows lurking around the corner.

You are allowed to experience unprecedented joy in this lifetime. Your wildest dreams may come true right in front of your eyes, and you are allowed to embrace them. You are allowed to know real peace, real love, real fulfillment. *You are allowed to be happy.* So please—don't close yourself off. Don't put up walls to block beautiful things from entering your life. Don't reject this gift the Universe has orchestrated just for you. When something beautiful wants to enter your life, let it in—because you are so incredibly deserving and more than enough.

On my hardest and heaviest days, I listen to the divine voice of love and allow it to **gently** guide me back to self-kindness, self-compassion, and **inner peace**.

On the really hard days, when you're struggling to do the most basic tasks, the world feels too heavy to hold, and your mind feels like an unkind place to be, take a deep breath. One long inhalation. Pause at the top. Full exhalation. And ask yourself—if *love* had a voice, what would it tell me right now? Love might say, *You've had a rough time lately and maybe you're having a hard time seeing yourself clearly right now, but I can see you. I see your courage and your heart. You are so much stronger and braver than you will ever realize.* Love might whisper, *You did it. You got out of bed and put one foot in front of the other, and you kept going. You made it through another day. And a small part of you wanted to just give up, but you didn't; I'm so proud of you.* Love might tell you, *It's okay to rest. It's okay to sit here and do nothing at all. It's okay if you just need to take time to breathe. I promise—you're safe here. You're safe to just be.*

Love might nudge you to be a little gentler with yourself today. To show yourself a little extra compassion. To pour your energy into your own vessel instead of giving it away to everyone else. Love might be your protector when the voice of self-criticism feels impossible to escape. *You are worthy*, it says firmly. *You are enough. Nothing about you is wrong; nothing about you is a mistake. You are perfectly and divinely made.* And sometimes love may simply remind you over and over: *You are loved. You are loved. You are loved.* Again and again without fail: *You are loved. You are loved. You are loved.* Sometimes, this is the only thing you need to remember. The only thing you need to hear. The only truth in the Universe that matters. *You are loved. You are loved. You are loved.*

I say yes to my **dreams**, my potential, and following my **passions** and excitement.

Say yes. When you feel that rush of excitement humming beneath your skin. When you see a shimmer of something beautiful—a flicker of possibility, a glimmer of hope—in the distance. When you hear a whisper inside you that says, *I think this might be for me.* Say yes to following the excitement, to moving toward what's being illuminated on the path ahead—to trusting that whisper. And when the question hovers at the tip of your tongue—*Can I really do this?*—Say yes. Yes, you can do it. Yes, you have what it takes. Yes, it's worth finding out where this journey might lead. Say yes to diving into your own potential and staying open to the idea that you might be much more capable than you think. Say yes to continuing on this path of truth and discovery and alignment. Keep saying yes.

There is an unknown road ahead of you. While you may not be able to predict its twists and turns or dictate its parameters, this much is true: If you say no to yourself and deny your own inner voice, you will continually remain right where you are. But when you say yes to experiencing life to the absolute fullest, life says yes back to you. The path will continue to unfold and expand. And while you may not know exactly where this road is taking you, because you have honored yourself, you will know that it will be rooted in love and authenticity. Saying yes is your soul's love language. It's a way of showing yourself that you are worthy of living a full, honest, exquisite life. So please—find the thing you want to say yes to today, and honor it with your whole heart.

I hold my **heart** with the gentle care and tenderness it deserves and acknowledge my **profound** inner strength.

You're fighting battles that no one knows about. You feel pain that nobody else can see. You've shed tears that no one has ever witnessed. There are parts of your story that nobody else will ever read. And you may think that you are weak on the days when all you can do is just breathe. But you don't realize how incredibly strong you truly are—and how much strength it takes to be gentle and tender with your heart. You are still spreading light to so many people, even on your darkest nights. You are a beacon of love and kindness and compassion. You feel pain but are careful not to spread that pain to others. And you may not see how special this is, because you feel like you have no other option. But you do.

The other option would be to give up. To let yourself become angry at the unfairness of life. To hurt others the way you've been hurt. But that's not you. You have a pure and gentle spirit. And the most profound gift you can give yourself is to learn how to hold your heart with the tender care and compassion it deserves. To allow yourself to see the beauty that radiates from your inner being and touches the world in the softest, most loving way. To know how precious this is, how courageous this is—how rare you truly are. You are blooming in the darkness—metamorphosing in the solitude of your cocoon. These dark nights won't last forever. But the love that you cultivate from within during these quiet moments will stay with you for the rest of your life.

I **gracefully** let go of anything that is no longer meant to remain in my life, making **space** for the right people, experiences, and **opportunities** to come forward.

You can't keep something that doesn't want to be kept. You can't cling to what's not meant to stay. You can't hold on to what's only meant to last for a season. No matter how much you love it, no matter how badly your heart wants it, no matter how precious it is to you—you can't force anything to remain where it is if its future isn't meant to be intertwined with yours. And if you're afraid to find out what will happen if you release it, that's exactly when it's time to let it go. If you're afraid it will leave, you must let it leave. If you're afraid it will choose a different path, you must allow it to do exactly that.

It's one of the hardest things you will ever do, but you must trust that what's meant to be yours *will* find you. That it *will* choose you as fiercely as you choose it. If it leaves and does not come back, know that this was not your only option—this was not your last chance. *This ending is not the end of your story.* There is more. So much more. And you're worthy of choosing the thing that chooses you—you're worthy of fighting for the thing that would fight for you. You're worthy of never having to ask, *Is this real? Is this reciprocated? Is this right?* This doesn't mean you have to forget the people and experiences that comprised your past. You can honor and feel grateful for what was once a meaningful and important part of your life. But please know—there is more. *There is more.*

I make **better** decisions and see the world more **clearly** when I give myself a chance to slow down.

At first, slowing down allows you to connect with your breath. Your blood pressure decreases. Your nervous system begins to calm down. A sense of relief permeates throughout your entire being. Then you start to notice the physical world with more clarity. The sights. The sounds. The experience of being truly alive and awake in this present moment. You turn your vision inward and begin to pay attention to what's happening inside you. Physically, you feel where you're holding on to tension within your body. Emotionally, you become aware of the underlying feelings that are coursing through you. Mentally, you become an observer of the thoughts that have been overpowering your mind.

Without thinking about it, something unexpected happens; the unseen becomes seen. The solution to the problem that's been haunting you. The alternate path you didn't realize was available. The creative spark you thought you had lost. A new understanding that alters your perspective on a situation. You can reflect upon the past day or the past month or even the past year and replay all the events that have occurred during that stretch of time—but suddenly you're telling a completely different story. Instead of a story of loss, it's a story of discovery. Instead of a story of breakdowns, it's a story of breakthroughs. Instead of a story of rejection, it's a story of redirection. All those times when it felt like the Universe was working against you, you can now see how it was working *for* you. A few minutes of slowing down can lead you to more meaningful discovery and growth than a week of constant striving, pursuing, and chasing. A month of solitude and silence can be more productive than a year of nonstop hustle. Lean into the slowdown. That's where you'll find what you're searching for.

I know that even when it **feels** like nothing is happening, the Universe is **always** working in the background to support me.

Right now, you can see what's in front of you. You can perceive what exists in your immediate surroundings. You can name the people who play a role in this chapter of your story. You know your past and present. You may also have some plans mapped out for the near future: places you will go, people you will see, experiences you will have. These are the details of the life that you know. But beyond that there is a life that you don't know, though it's part of your story too.

There are things happening in this world beyond your scope of vision. Things that seemingly have no direct connection to you: a conversation that is happening, a decision that is being made, a new path being forged. Every person's journey is a distinct thread in the fabric of the Universe. And right now, there are threads that have never crossed with yours. But they will. So much that you cannot see is happening in this world. Even when it feels like nothing is happening, something *is* happening. Soon it will be brought to light. The person you will be meeting. The opportunity that will be arriving. The miracle that is on its way. The Universe is weaving these threads together in carefully orchestrated timing, one intersecting with another until suddenly it happens: the right one crosses yours, and your life alters in the most extraordinary way. Keep your heart open to the possibility that, in any moment, your thread can cross with another's, and your journey will be forever changed. The most breathtaking things often find you when you least expect them. What's happening in the background is part of your story too. In this very moment, even though you cannot yet see it, the Universe is conspiring in your favor.

There is beauty in contrast. My darkest nights and most difficult challenges **illuminate** my profound inner strength and guide me toward a deeper sense of **appreciation** for all that I have.

Everything in the world has an opposite. Hot and cold. Fast and slow. Night and day. One cannot exist without the other. Polarity is everywhere—it's a core tenet of this Universe. It shows up in the rainy and sunny days. It shows up in the periods of good health and of illness. It shows up in the first hellos and the last goodbyes. And within these contrasts, there are lessons and messages to be uncovered.

Because you've lived through the worst days of your life, you can feel an even deeper and richer appreciation for the beautiful ones. The darkest nights of your life have led you to unearth a deep inner strength and power you didn't know you possessed, fortifying the trust you now have in yourself. You've worked some terrible jobs, tolerated other people's selfish behavior, and have gone to places where you never quite felt like you belonged. Through these experiences, you've learned more about yourself, what truly matters, and what you will never tolerate again. Even deeper: The existence of polarity offers a spark of hope. You know that everything has an opposite, and eventually you realize that there are many experiences beyond the boundaries of what you know. Experiences that are the very opposite of what you have experienced. You may know heartbreak, but gentle and enduring love exists. You may know loneliness, but there is true community and companionship available in this world for you. It is all real and attainable. Every bad, hard, difficult experience you've lived through has an opposite. There is love, connection, triumph, exhilaration, and hope. There are honest people, celebratory moments, and places that know how to hold your heart the way it deserves. All the darker moments will lead to lighter ones, if you stay open to them.

I **nurture** my inner child with my **wholehearted** attention and **unconditional** love and support.

Your inner child is part of you. They hold every experience you lived through and every emotion you felt when you were younger. Some of the memories you carry are filled with unbridled joy. Your inner child remembers what it's like to imagine, play, and create. They are filled with curiosity and wonder. They're the part of you that still believes in magic and sees the world as vast and unlimited, but they also carry deep-rooted wounds. There may have been words you desperately wanted to hear when you were younger but never did. You may have craved attention, not because you were selfish but because you just wanted someone to show you that you were important and valuable—that you mattered. Or maybe you just wanted someone to listen—to truly care about what you had to say.

One of the most profound healing experiences comes when you choose to nurture your inner child as a loving parent would. Sometimes, this looks like being their companion on an adventure. Or you may ask them what they want to say—and then truly listen to their words the way you wished someone would have listened to you when you were younger. Sometimes, it means speaking the words they most need to hear: *You are safe. You are loved. You are never going to be alone again.* As you make space to love and nurture your inner child, you'll find that the current, grown-up version of you—the you who is physically older but still longs for the same things you wanted back then—will feel the burden you've been carrying get a little smaller and your innermost pain become a little lighter. You heal by uplifting, protecting, and caring for your inner child the way you've always deserved.

I remain **committed**, consistent, and courageous, **no matter** what.

Create a vision board. Write yourself a letter. Keep a picture of your younger self somewhere in close reach. Come back to these things every time you think about giving up on your dreams, your quest for self-love, or whatever it is that is bringing you meaning. Remember your *why*—why you started, why you keep showing up, why it's worth it. Remember who you're doing this for: for your younger self. For your future self. *For you.* You're not doing this to prove anything or impress anyone, or for glory or accolades. You're doing it for every version of *you* you've ever been. You're doing it because you owe it to your younger self to build them a life filled with peace, contentment, joy, and love. You're doing it because every past and future version of you deserves to know what it feels like when a dream comes true. You're doing it because *you matter*. Your voice, words, and ideas matter.

If you can offer your authentic self to the world, if you can step forward and make the spaces around you a little brighter with your inner light, if you can create even the tiniest glimmer of hope and positivity in the Universe—then maybe you can make a bigger impact on this world than you even realize. Maybe the things you *do* and *say* will have a ripple effect that extends far beyond what you will ever see. And maybe you can make yourself—every version of yourself you've ever been and ever will be—proud. This is why you remain committed, consistent, and courageous, no matter what. Because you can create the life that every past and future version of you deserves to live; because you have the power to make the world around you look and feel a little more beautiful.

I **courageously** follow the path that feels right to me, **regardless** of how it looks to others.

The right path is often going to be the hard one. It's going to be the one that requires you to believe in something that comes with no guarantees. It's going to be the one that asks you to offer up your heart, with the risk that it might break. The right path is going to call for you to let go of the reins—to walk forward in what other people might call blind faith. But deep down, you know you're not walking blindly. Deep down, you know—there's no other choice but *this*. This uncertain road. This unmarked trail. And the right path—it's going to be the one that starts with only a tiny nudge. A strange, unexplainable pull. A stirring deep inside your soul. It's the consciousness that exists not inside your head but within your heart. It's an untouchable inner wisdom that nobody can take away. It's *yours* to feel, hear, and honor. And often, the right path is going to be the one that scares you. It's going to rattle your insides. It's going to be the opposite of a sure thing.

None of this means that choosing this path will be stressful or difficult. Because there will also be that inherent feeling—that intangible knowing—that *this is it*. That this is *for you*. And even on your hardest days, you'll know there's nothing truer or more real—nothing you'd rather fight for—than *this*. So please, find the thing that excites and terrifies you, that may feel uncertain but also feels *meaningful*, *honest*, and *true*. And when you find it, when you sense it, when you know with every fiber of your being, *This is real* and *This is right* and *This is for me*, don't deny it for anyone or anything.

I can **release** my worries because I know everything is always working out for me **exactly** as it's meant to.

One of the most freeing realizations you'll ever have is when you can look at the path ahead of you and confidently say, *The outcome doesn't matter.* This doesn't mean you don't have wants and desires or you don't feel excitement about the possibilities in front of you. It also doesn't mean you aren't reaching for the things that your heart is being pulled to and hoping they reach back. It means that you're standing on a foundation built on trust. And you know, if this doesn't work out exactly the way you hope, it's because there's something coming that's even more perfectly aligned. If the path you're on doesn't lead to the place you're dreaming about, it's because it's leading you somewhere you haven't even begun to dream about. If *this one opportunity* doesn't work out, there's another, even better one coming. If *this one person* isn't meant to stay in your life, the right person—*the person you can't even imagine right now*—will show up in your life at the exact right time.

Ultimately, you understand that the Universe is always on your side—that there are things happening behind the scenes that you can't yet see. And if you don't get *exactly what you want* in this moment, you know you're still always getting *exactly what you need*. It means you know that what's meant for you will not miss you—that divine timing is real and it's always working in your favor. The greatest freedom is when you can say with wholehearted belief, *The outcome doesn't matter.* You know the revealed path will be even greater than the one you've created in your mind—that you can let go, surrender, and trust the unfolding.

What is meant for me **chooses** me, wholeheartedly **reciprocates** my energy, and feels effortlessly **aligned.**

If it isn't meant for you, you can't force it. And if it *is* meant for you, you can't chase it away. Please remember that. On the hard days. On the heavy days. On the days when you feel like you're not worthy or good enough. What's meant for you isn't fickle. It doesn't waver. It doesn't require that you reach the pinnacle of perfection to earn it, have it, keep it. What's meant for you isn't for you only once you're fully healed. It doesn't stand beside you only when you're at your very best. What's meant for you isn't fleeting. It's not transitory. You won't push it away by being *too much* or *not enough*. You'll never have to chase it or beg it to choose you. If it's meant for you, it won't have to be convinced. What's meant for you will fight for you as hard as you fight for it and will choose you as wholeheartedly as you choose it. And it will feel effortlessly aligned—inevitable, even. Like this is how it was always meant to be. Like the long and uncertain path you've been walking upon for so long was always destined to lead to this person, this place, this experience—to this thing that is so much better than what you had envisioned. For so many years, you fought to prove your worthiness. But you don't need to prove your worth to your destined matches. Because what's meant for you already thinks you're worthy. It already knows that you're enough. As you climb your highest mountains and descend into your deepest valleys, it will walk with you and hold your hand and remain by your side. And it will stay. *It will stay.*

I **attract** the right people into my life when I offer my **authentic** self to the world and allow my truest inner light to shine.

In the past, you may have believed that it was your job to convince people of your value. You may have thought that you needed to perform for someone's attention or prove your worth to attract the connections and relationships you've always dreamed about. But this is a false belief. To manifest a life surrounded by the right people, all you need to do is stay true to yourself, remain faithful to your own heart, and allow your inner light to shine. This may sound easy enough in theory, but it can be one of the most terrifying things you ever do. It can feel far scarier to give people a glimpse into *the real you* than to offer a curated, false version of yourself to the world—because it means allowing others to truly see you and trusting that they won't run away. But this is how you attract the right people into your life and open yourself up to manifesting friendships that flourish, business partnerships rooted in honesty and trust, and romantic relationships that feel loving and secure.

Define what it means for you to be your authentic self. Ask yourself what your inner light is composed of—maybe it's your soft and gentle demeanor, or maybe it's your lively and exuberant spirit—and vow to offer that genuine part of you to every experience you walk into. As you do this, trust that you don't need to perform or prove yourself to the people who are meant for you. When you allow your inner light to radiate, you become a magnet for people whose hearts and energy match yours. Allow yourself to risk being rejected by the wrong people to attract the right ones—the people who *want* to see you shine.

I am **complete** as I am, and everything that makes me different is everything that makes me **perfectly** and beautifully me.

It can be easy to get lost in that feeling—the feeling of being different. The feeling that something inside you must be broken. The feeling of always being an outsider. When you watch the people around you embarking upon their paths, it feels like everyone else has it all figured out. They can navigate the world. They've discovered the secret of how to thrive, be happy, and feel whole. But you never quite feel like you fit in anywhere. It can often feel like you're staying in the same place while everyone else is moving forward and building big, impressive lives. Sometimes you think you are *too much*. Other times, you're convinced you're *not enough*. You magnify the characteristics you judge as *wrong* and try to find ways to somehow overcome them—like if you could just figure out a way to defeat these parts of yourself, you'd finally be able to find your place in this world.

However, it's exactly the distinctive qualities that you deem *wrong* that make you perfectly, magnificently *you*. Yes, you're different, but it's not in a way that makes you strange and incompatible with other people. You're different in a way that makes you unique and rare. You're different in a way that makes you wholly compatible with *exactly the right people*. When you lean into your differences and begin to hold your own heart like it's precious and irreplaceable—*when you fall in love with the entirety of yourself*—you become magnetic. Your quirks and eccentricities will find homes with hearts that fit with yours. Your place in this world will be revealed, and you won't need to hide a single part of you to belong. Because nothing about you is broken. Nothing about you needs to be hidden. Nothing about you is a mistake. You are fully complete, and everything that makes you different is everything that makes you beautiful, brilliant, and incomparable.

I set and **maintain** personal boundaries that are **firmly** rooted in love and self-respect.

Sometimes you must set personal boundaries; your personal time belongs to you. Even though it may look like Tuesday evenings are open on your schedule, those nights are reserved for self-care: for reading, painting, watching a show, or *whatever it is that your soul needs*. Sometimes, the boundary you must set in your life is that you will not dedicate the entirety of your time and energy to work. That you will not take on too many hours or too many projects. That you will not get so caught up in the busyness of each workday that you don't take breaks. Sometimes, the boundary you must set in your life is that certain conversation topics are off-limits. You won't discuss deeply personal matters with anyone outside of a chosen group of trusted people. You won't engage in gossip that is meant to demean others. Maybe romantic relationships can only progress at a speed you feel comfortable with, or highly charged, emotional conversations must be approached under specific conditions. Sometimes the boundary is that your personal space must be respected. Sometimes it's that you will not maintain a relationship with anyone who tries to convince you to act against your values and beliefs.

In every area of your life, boundaries are essential. Because at the core of every single boundary you set is *love*. Love for yourself. Love for the relationships that are important to you. Love for life itself and how you deserve to experience it deeply, fully, and in alignment with your heart's truths. Set boundaries that are rooted in love. Make them the pillars of your life. What dies because of your personal boundaries was never meant to last. But what remains—those things will not just survive but bloom.

I remain **loyal** to my heart and honor my **soul's** calling above all else.

At times, you will have to be brave enough to say, *I don't accept that story.* When somebody tells you that your dream isn't possible. When they try to convince you to follow a path that *they* think is safer and more predictable than the one you feel pulled toward. When they try to talk you out of what you know in your *mind* and *body* and *soul* is right. You will have to be brave enough to say, *That may be your belief, but it's not mine.* Someone may have good intentions. They may love you. They may want the best for you. But they don't realize that they're projecting their own stories onto you. They may know a lifetime of nonstop work and hustle, so they don't agree when you tell them you're going to prioritize rest; they may not understand that to help others, you first need to help yourself. Their priority may be financial abundance while yours may be something completely different: a desire to connect more deeply with the earth, a yearning for adventure, or a pull to explore creative endeavors. And they very likely don't see the vision you can see. They can't feel what you can feel. They don't know the relationship you have with your higher self, with the Universe, with life itself. When someone asks you to go against your own heart, they're asking you to betray the core of who you are. They may not realize this. They may simply want to keep you safe. But there comes a day when you have to be brave enough to ask for freedom. Freedom to make your own rules. To write your own story. To choose your own path. Because no matter what anyone else tells you, you must not betray your own heart.

I give **myself** permission to sit with my pain, anger, grief, and sadness for as long as I need to **without** judgment or self-criticism.

It's okay if you're not ready to find the silver lining in a difficult experience. There's wisdom in uncovering the light in the darkness, but sometimes it's okay to just *be* in the darkness for a little while. To not self-help your way out of what you're experiencing. To feel every single bit of anger, pain, grief, and sadness—*to feel it all*—without trying to force yourself into a mindset of positivity. And it's okay if all you can do today is just breathe. It's okay if today you need to leave the lessons for your future self to uncover. And maybe in the future, when it feels right, you'll be able to find one small thing. One spark of hope. One lifelong lesson. Even if that one thing is *I never knew I could be so strong*.

However, right now, it's okay to feel what you need to feel. To be here, exactly where you are, without judging yourself. Your pain is worth honoring, and you don't need to rush through it. Go at your own pace. Give yourself grace. Life can be gut-wrenching and overwhelming and unfair. And right now, you might just need to be angry or sad. You might need to shut your blinds and hide from the world, and it's okay if you're not okay. It's okay if you can't put on a happy face, or if everything feels heavy and you don't want to be the model for positive thinking. Maybe one day you'll look back on today and see this experience differently. But you don't need to rush to get to that point. Just be here where you are, allowing space for every single emotion that comes to light. That is all you need to do when the world feels too heavy to bear.

I can feel **grateful** for my past while not clinging to it too **tightly**, because I know there is an even more beautiful **future** awaiting up ahead.

You've already lived so many lives within this single lifetime. You have a rich, intricate history. There have been days in your life that passed by so quietly you may never think of them again. Others are imprinted in your memory and impossible to forget. And still—for all the years that have passed, the goodbyes you've said, and the beautiful and devastating and wondrous days you've lived—there is still so much life ahead of you. And there is still so much love here for you.

Some of your best days haven't even come yet. Some of your favorite people, you haven't yet met. Some of your greatest chapters—they're still being written. And one day you're going to look back and see that life was guiding you and preparing you for something more stunning than you ever knew existed. That it was always on your side, working in your favor. Weaving together a unique tapestry that was so much richer and more vibrant than you had ever allowed yourself to imagine. You have experienced so much in this lifetime, and *there is still so much more coming*. So much more to experience. An entire future to explore. You're right on time and exactly where you need to be. The Universe doesn't miss. And what's coming—you won't need to force it. Because it's going to settle deep inside your bones. And you're not just going to *survive* the years to come—you're going to *flourish*.

My hard work, kindness, and **self-belief** will continue to take me farther than I can **possibly** imagine.

The simplest things will take you farthest in life. The most straightforward approach is the one that works time and time again. First, when you find the thing you feel called to do, you work really hard at it. But it's not the type of hard work that leaves you feeling miserable and unfulfilled; it isn't consuming your energy without offering anything in return. It's hard work that feels meaningful and purposeful. It feels good, like it's what you were put on this earth to do. And as you continue to work hard, you will meet many people along the way. Some can help you, but it doesn't matter what they can offer you. What matters is that you offer the same thing to every single person you encounter, no matter who they are: kindness.

To be truly kind, you must start with yourself. You must pour love and kindness into yourself so you can give with the overflow. Because this isn't simply about being nice, which can feel forced and disingenuous; your true kindness is genuine. And people can feel that kindheartedness when they're with you; they feel a sense of safety in your presence. You can only offer that depth of kindness when you've walked into your own shadows and learned how to offer compassion to the most wounded parts of your innermost self. Finally, as you continue to work hard and treat people with kindness, *you believe*. You believe in yourself and your dreams. You believe that the Universe is on your side. That everything you do today matters—that it's all paying off in ways you can't even imagine. Hard work, kindness, and self-belief. It is these three simple things that will take you farthest in life. It's these three basic principles that you cannot abandon.

The **best** time to
follow my heart
is **right now.**

The best time to follow your heart is not when everything is perfectly aligned and you finally feel like you're ready; the best time is right now, *always*. The best time to follow your heart is when you realize that you haven't been. Sometimes, following your heart means taking a risk: making a declaration, performing a grand gesture, doing something that feels like it could change *everything*. But quite often it means simply taking the tiniest step in a direction you've never walked in before. It means listening to the soft nudge inside you. Following that nudge. And then the next one. And the next one. Moving slowly as you build a life that feels like it doesn't take from your years but *gives you more*.

Make space to listen to your heart every day. Settle into stillness, even if for just a few minutes. Feel into your heart center. Ask it what it wants you to know. Be willing to believe that you have something inside you that is more powerful and possesses more wisdom than you even realize—and, even more, be willing to trust it. Because that *thing* you feel is on your side, and it wants to lead you to your happiness on this earth. There are no do-overs of this life you're living. There is only right now. And right now, in this present moment—this is where your power exists. Not in the past. Not in the future. Right now. That is all there is. *And it is not too late.* The best time to fall in love with your life is today. The best time to choose your path is this moment. The best time to create something truly stunning with the years you have in front of you is *right now*.

Instead of **focusing** on limits and boundaries, I see **potential** and possibilities.

If there is one place where you should allow yourself to feel completely limitless, it is in your imagination. Start there. Begin building your life in your mind's eye. Continually allow yourself to extend the boundaries of what you can see just *a little bit farther* than you ever have before. Your success is bigger. Your abundance is greater. Your love is deeper. You cultivate even truer connections. The colors of the world around you look and feel more vibrant. And there are *unlimited* paths to explore. In your imagination, you get to follow your curiosity and investigate these paths without fear. You get to try on different lives without commitment. So explore them fully. Maybe one path leads you to a life in the city. Another leads you to the ocean. Another leads you to the forest. Play in these worlds. You may come out of each one realizing it doesn't feel right for you—but that's the entire point: the simple but life-changing realization that you are not limited to a single path—*that you have options*.

Keep exploring the infinite possibilities that are available to you, because one day you're going to explore a path that *does* feel right. One day, you're going to reach for something completely unexpected and realize it's reaching back—that it wants you as deeply as you want it. And everything will start to shift, simply because you were willing to dismantle the limits you once imposed on yourself. Life opens for you when you choose to view the world through a lens of possibilities rather than boundaries. Everything will feel conceivable, and nothing will seem out of reach. It all starts within, right where you are. It starts with uncovering the limitlessness inside yourself and making it your unshakeable truth.

I reject, **deny**, and turn away from anything that asks me to be a less **true** version of myself.

What is your current life asking of you? Who is it asking you to be? Is it asking you to be the truest, most loving version of yourself, to *just be you*? It's unavoidable: Throughout your life, you'll encounter people and experiences that will ask you to be a less true version of yourself. Some will only want you to fill a specific role in their lives without caring that *who they want you to be* isn't *who you are*. Some will treat you as though you are just a number or placeholder. There will even be periods in which every aspect of the life you're living feels wrong—where you are, what you're doing, who you're surrounded by. In some ways, these experiences can be opportunities for self-discovery and personal growth. They teach you about yourself and the world. They provide the contrast needed to guide you toward what you *do* want as you continue your journey of creating a life you love. But these experiences are only meant to be temporary. You are not meant to create a life in an environment that asks you to be a less true version of yourself. Your roots will never flourish in hostile soil; your petals will never fully expand.

When something new enters your life, notice how your energy responds. Notice how it makes you feel. Notice if it feels like it's bringing you closer to your authentic self or pulling you farther away. Be willing to walk away from anything that asks you to become a less true version of yourself to fit. Because it's out there: the right person, the right place, the right opportunity, the feeling of belonging. The feeling of *home*. And if you're willing to choose yourself, the right things will come along and choose you too.

Instead of **looking** to the outside world for answers, I **listen** to the voice of my highest self.

What inspires you when you paint a picture of the most honest and beautiful life you can imagine for yourself? What excites you when you let go of other people's opinions and focus solely on the things that genuinely light you up inside? What ignites a spark in your heart? Where would you go if you could go anywhere? How would you show up in the world if you allowed yourself to be *all that you are*? The answers to these questions lead you to your highest self—to your inner guide, to your innate wisdom, to the part of you that *just knows*.

Your highest self knows what's right for you. They know what's real. They can lead you to your deepest truths and guide you to your purest joy. And they are the single voice whose beliefs and opinions matter more than any other. If you can't hear this voice, then allow yourself to make space for them. Within the stillness, visualize your highest self: the *you* who lives through the heart and knows deep love, happiness, serenity, and freedom. How do they look and speak? How do they carry themself? Picture them in a place where you feel most at peace: by the ocean, among the trees, in a meadow of wildflowers. As they look you in the eyes, feel the deep, enduring, unconditional love they have for you. There's no judgment, no criticism, no fault finding. Only love. Ask them what they want you to know. Hear their words in your heart center. Return to this vision throughout your days. When you need to decide your path, go to your highest self. Ask them for guidance. They hold the blueprint to your future and have the answers; they know the way.

I am **deeply,**
fully, and
unconditionally
loved.

Always. You were always loved. In every version of this body you've lived in. Through all the transformations. While you were unraveling. While you were desperately trying to pick up the pieces of the person you once were. When some of those pieces got left behind. When you didn't know how to love yourself—you were loved. You were loved even when you were convinced you weren't worth loving. You were loved even when you wanted to shatter the reflection staring back at you in the mirror. You were loved even when you were haunted by your darkest thoughts. Always. You were always loved.

It's a beautiful thing when you can finally accept and realize that even as you're healing, *you are loved*. Love isn't the prize you receive for curing the wounds inside you—the wounds that you've hidden to appear okay, believing that they somehow make you lesser, and believing that if other people saw them they'd think less of you too. It's a beautiful thing to understand that this was never true. To realize that even as you're healing, love will stay with you, and it will hold you like you are the most delicate, precious thing. This love will walk with you on your journey as you retreat or fall apart, or as you find the strength inside yourself to face another day. You do not need to wait until the storm is over to be loved; even as the wind is blowing and the thunder is roaring and the rain is pouring down on you, love is with you. Always. Through every chapter of your story. Every single time you've ever felt lost and uncertain of your place in this world, your heart was always seen. Your soul was always known. You have always been loved.

I **choose** to go all in on myself, my goals, and my **dreams**.

By going all in on yourself, you create the life you've always wanted. You listen to that quiet voice within, the soft nudges, the whisper of your intuition—to that *thing* deep inside you that *just knows*. You trust your inner knowing and honor what feels right, even when it scares you. And when the voice of fear asks, *But what if it doesn't work out?* you choose to listen to the voice of belief that responds, *But what if it does?*

You remind yourself every single day that your spirit is irrepressible. That you are brave, capable, and incredibly strong. Everything you need to follow your heart-led path *already exists within you*. You stay true to yourself and choose yourself every single day. You never turn your back on your own beating heart. You do this consistently and deliberately—because you know that *time passes by so fast*. And you might as well spend it doing what you love. Being brave. Risking your heart. Going all in on the things that make you feel alive. You spend time falling in love with people, places, and new experiences. You cherish this soft, strong, stubborn heart that beats inside your chest. And if there's an uncharted path that calls to you, *you take it*. If there's a pull in your heart guiding you forward, *you follow it*. If there's a vision that you see every time you close your eyes, *you honor and trust it*. You feel every ounce of fear and step forward anyway. Because you know that some things are worth it. The crucial things, *the things that you can feel deep down in your bones*, they're worth risking it all for. They're worth fighting for. They're worth living for.

I honor my body by **trusting** the signals that it sends me and **treating** it with respect.

Your relationship with your body is sacred and personal. Only you know what is right for it and can hear its subtlest signals. You alone know what it needs. Treating your body with respect often means feeding it nourishing foods that offer it the nutrients it craves. It may mean moving it in ways that feel good to you or even pushing it beyond the limits of what you thought it could handle. Lifting a heavier weight. Running an extra mile. Adding five more minutes to your workout. However, this is *not* the only way to honor your body. Sometimes, showing your body respect means allowing it to rest and going a little easier on yourself. Sleeping in when you're feeling utterly exhausted. Being gentle instead of pushing it further.

Even more, treating your body with respect is about remembering that your physical vessel is more than just your outer appearance. It is the home where your mind, heart, soul, and energy all reside. It is the wholeness of you. You honor your body by practicing self-care that sustains each of these invaluable parts of your innermost self. And how this looks and feels to you can change every single day. So to truly honor your body, inside and out, you must continually check in with yourself and learn the language that it speaks. What is it telling you today? If your energy feels restless, it might be telling you that it needs movement and exercise. If there's an unexplainable sadness within, you might need sunshine or a coffee date with a friend. If your bones feel heavy, you may simply need rest. Whatever it's telling you, honor your body's message by listening when it speaks.

I **possess** the skills, talent, and knowledge to do everything I've been called to do, and I am **deserving** of my success.

One of the biggest lies you will ever tell yourself is that your success is a result of luck. When you're in a room filled with influential people, you might feel like you're not one of them—like you don't deserve to be there. A small voice in your head might worry that someone will look at you and call you out as a fraud. In those moments, it can be easy to forget what you've accomplished. It's easy to lose sight of the fact that it wasn't good luck that brought you here today; it's your knowledge, skills, and talent that led you here. It's your dedication, commitment, and consistency. It's *you*. *You* are the reason you're here. *You* are the reason for your success—and you are deserving of every bit of it.

When you begin to feel like an impostor—if any part of you feels like you don't deserve the praise, accolades, or success you've received—think back upon every late night and early morning you spent working hard to accomplish your goals. Remember the hours dedicated to perfecting your craft. Recall every milestone that led you here today. If it helps, write down a list of each step you've taken to reach this point, and read it every time you feel like you're not good enough. You're here because you deserve to be here. You've earned the praise you've received. You've made it this far because *you have what it takes*. You are not an impostor. You are not a fraud. You didn't stumble your way into this position. The knowledge you've accumulated, the skills you've refined, and the talent you've fine-tuned through consistent hard work have led you to where you are today. So when success finds you, know that *you deserve it.*

I release any limiting **beliefs** that are holding me back from **stepping toward** my dreams.

Limiting beliefs are not true unless you allow them to be. The reasons you supposedly *can't* or *shouldn't* do something only hold as much power as you allow. The limiting boundaries you set may establish what's possible, what you're capable of, and what you're allowed to have and receive in this lifetime, but they are not unalterable. They only exist for as long as you allow them to exist. Every belief you uphold and build your life around is only that—a belief. Not a fact. Think about your biggest dreams. Think about your quietest aspirations. Think about what your heart longs for more than anything else. What's stopping you from stepping toward what you desire? What are the beliefs you cling to that prevent you from even trying? Now, dig even deeper. Look for the stories that were passed down to you by family, society, and the world—stories you don't have to claim as yours if they don't feel right to you.

You may have heard that you must work to the point of burnout to succeed in life, or that your worthiness is defined by your achievements. Perhaps you've thought about what *is* and *isn't* possible for someone like you. Write it all down: every false story and limiting belief you possess. Flip it upside down. Make it an affirmation. *I'm not talented enough to make it* becomes *I have exactly what it takes to succeed and thrive. Nobody will love me the way I am* becomes *I have many amazing qualities to offer and am worthy of being loved exactly as I am. I can't* becomes *I can and I will.* Create new stories from the old limiting beliefs you once carried. Make these your new pillars. Choose them every day.

I **remain** patient, positive, and persistent in the **pursuit** of my goals.

Good things take time. And the *really* good things? They're worth the wait. The dream you feel so connected to that it feels as real as the breath that flows through your lungs. The vision that draws you in so powerfully that it feels as though you can reach out and touch it. The sky-high goals and aspirations you've set for yourself. Sometimes the vision seems far away. And you tell yourself that you should be doing something to force it to come quicker. But force is not the answer. Trying to work *against* the current of life will not get you what you desire any faster. Instead, it's about setting healthy and achievable goals that get you there one step at a time.

Think about what's taking place behind the scenes, the events transpiring in the background that you can't yet see. Those take time to unfold, and the unfolding is worth your patience and trust. Don't try to force what's meant for you. Look within yourself for the map and guidance that will show you the way and figure out which goals are uplifting you toward your dreams. Once you're on your way, your inner rhythm tells you the pace at which to move. So trust what you feel. Keep nurturing the seeds you've planted. Keep listening to your own energy—resting when you feel called to rest, leaping when it feels right to leap. Keep releasing and receiving. The most stunning things find you when you least expect them. You're not missing out or losing out on anything. When your goals come into focus and create your dream, you'll know—it was always worth the wait.

Even when the future looks uncertain, I can find the **gift** the Universe is offering me in this **present** moment.

Find the gift. Sometimes, that is all you can do. When worry hits or fear takes over. When your mind asks the same questions, replays the same worst-case scenarios, and pokes and prods for every possible thing that might go wrong. *What if this opportunity doesn't work out? What if this person doesn't feel the same way? What if this good thing that's happening ends abruptly?* Step back. Breathe. *Find the gift.* You can't control the world outside yourself. You can't choose what stays and what goes. You don't get to decide how every concurrent storyline of your life will play out. But you can find the gift that the Universe is offering you through this experience, regardless of how the story unfolds.

Maybe your fear is that a person you care for immensely will one day leave. And maybe the gift is that this person is showing you the depth of connection that exists when you open yourself up. Maybe your fear is that an opportunity you badly want won't work out. The gift could be what this process is teaching you and how it's aiding your personal growth. Maybe your fear is that you're not good enough for the thing you desire most. And maybe the gift is that this experience is offering you the opportunity to challenge and question the root of your fears. By questioning your fears, you can begin to release them. *Find the gift.* Sometimes that is all you can do. When your mind is so worried about what might be taken from you, allow yourself to notice what you're being given. What is the gift that is being offered to you through this experience? Find the gift. Focus on the gift. Let that be your anchor.

My greatest **impact** on this world is measured not by what I achieve but by how my **energy** and presence make others feel.

Some days, you will accomplish nothing on your to-do list. But you will drop everything to meet a friend for coffee because, in their lowest moment, they called only you. And you will hold their hand and be the reason why they feel *a little more seen* and *a little more valued* and *a little less alone*. Some weeks, you will not be the model of efficiency and productivity. But you will connect with your inner child and make space to *play* and *create*. You will reunite with your joyful innermost self, and your joy will radiate and touch those around you, bringing lightness to their lives too. Some months, you will not climb any mountains or set new personal records. But you will finally allow yourself to slow down, rest, and truly feel your heartbeat for the first time in so long. And this time you spend nursing your deepest wounds will be the catalyst to your powerful transformation. Afterward, you will be better equipped to help others heal, because you have taken that path already. You will be able to lead people to their joy because you allowed yourself the time to find yours.

One day, you will take the thing that was once your deepest wound and turn your pain into your purpose and become the person you needed all along. You will transmute your deepest hurt into your deepest love. And you will illuminate the darkness you've walked through with your own inner light. The value of some days, weeks, and months cannot be determined by how productive or efficient you were. They can't be measured by how many tasks you completed or goals you reached. The value of some periods of time can only be determined by the lives you touched and transformed—starting with your own.

I **choose** to walk
my highest path,
which is **anchored**
in peace, trust,
gratitude, and love.

When you're on your highest path, you'll know. You'll know by the lightness of your being and the ease of your breathing. You'll know by the peace you feel deep in your bones. You won't feel a desire to control what's happening around you or worry about the direction or pace in which you're moving. You'll sense with every cell of your being that everything is working out in your favor—that you can surrender, trust, and let go. When you're on your highest path, you won't live in your mind, replaying events of the past or obsessively worrying about the future. You'll be here, right now. With this breath. This heartbeat. Alive and present in this moment. Plus, the connections you make won't trigger your deepest insecurities. You won't expend your energy trying to convince anyone to see your worth. You'll never worry about concealing certain aspects of yourself or trying to be someone you're not, just to be liked. Every deep and enduring bond you build will be rooted in authenticity, acceptance, and love. As soon as someone crosses your path who is less than completely genuine, you'll be able to feel it—and you'll walk away with strength, grace, and ease.

Ultimately, your life will feel honest. It won't be dictated by someone else's rules or stories about what an acceptable life is *supposed* to look like. It will be built on your own values, your own principles, and your own beliefs. When you're on your highest path, you'll know because everything you pour energy into will pour energy back into you. You'll know by the deep appreciation you feel every morning and every night. You'll know, because of all the paths you could follow and all the lives you could live, you would choose this one without fail, every single time.

I take **care** of the future by taking care of the present **moment**.

How do I make the present moment as beautiful as it can possibly be? This is the question that will guide you in creating your future. It begins within. It begins with gratitude and paying attention. Your heart beats, lungs expand, mind thinks deep thoughts, and all of that is a miracle. You can perceive the world around you. You possess the ability to observe, make your own judgments, and form your own opinions. You are alive, here, and whole. And those are miracles. The world around you in all its shapes, colors, and movements; the flow of nature; the current of life; the existence of *all of this*—this planet, spinning in the middle of space in this infinite Universe, as stardust flows through your blood, breath, and bones. *Miracles.*

You take care of the future by treating this moment as precious. You are planting seeds that will one day bloom in the world outside of you. Pay attention to what you're planting. Carefully nurture and cultivate what you want to see grow. Love blooms when you create a caring environment within and give generously with the surplus that flows through your soul. Joy blooms when you follow your excitement and reach for the things that make you feel vibrant and alive and free. Peace blooms when you press your hand against your heart and exhale your worries and allow the earth beneath you to gently hold you in its loving embrace. Even more stunning things to adore and appreciate will bloom when you focus on the feeling of true gratitude for all that you have in this moment. Be here now. This is where your power exists. This is where the seeds to your future are sowed. This is the beginning of the rest of your life.

I am **breathtakingly** beautiful, inside and out.

Your beauty is your heart, your love, and your genuine and profound caring for others. Your beauty is how you make people feel when they're with you. It's the energy you radiate that causes another to intuitively know that they are *seen* and *safe* in your presence. It's the warmth you emit that makes them feel wanted when you're near. Your beauty is the light you carry that draws people in when they feel as though they're lost and alone in the middle of an endless ocean; it's the illumination of love that guides them back to the shore. Your beauty is your compassion and empathy. Your beauty is your willingness to step outside yourself to see what another sees, to feel what another feels, to know the world as they know it. Your beauty is your pure kindness. Your beauty is your enduring faith. Every gorgeous sight you admire in the world around you is simply a reflection of the beauty that *is* you.

Celebrate your beauty through your joy, courage, thoughtfulness, and generosity. The way you go through life, always trying to leave everything a little better than you found it—it is beautiful. Love your open and effortless giving, and honor your gifts of time and attention to the people in your life. Celebrate that you'd give the clothes off your back without question, without hesitation, and without ever asking for anything in return. These are the qualities that make you breathtakingly beautiful. Your beauty is your determination, never giving up on what's important or abandoning hope. Your beauty is your unique aura. It's your inner glow. It's the unrepeatable blueprint that makes you *you*. Your beauty is your divine essence. Your beauty is your irreplaceable spirit. Your beauty is your rare and remarkable soul.

I honor the lessons and **memories** of my past experiences while continuing to believe in my **vision** for a beautiful future.

Sometimes, a final goodbye comes suddenly and unexpectedly. Without any warning, the visions you had for tomorrow are taken from you before you're ready. You're left with grief, anger, and a myriad of emotions that you haven't even begun to unpack. Each one of your feelings is valid, but if any part of you feels like you've wasted time by investing your energy into a story that didn't end in *happily ever after*, please remember—just because something doesn't last forever doesn't make it a failure. People often measure success with statistics, as though a simple number can tell the whole story. But numbers can only tell you quantity; they don't reveal quality. They don't show how you grew as a person through this chapter of your journey. How you became braver. Wiser. Stronger yet softer. More in touch with your heart's softest whispers. Less willing to accept anything other than exactly what your soul needs to flourish.

Maybe this part of your story didn't last forever, but did it teach you about life, about the world, about yourself? Perhaps your journey of self-discovery and personal growth was worth the heartache, and you can now honor the memories of your past while moving forward. Even if it wasn't forever, if the goodbye was painful, or if you wish you could take some things back, you may be able to view the chapter's unfolding and ending through a lens of appreciation. Can you recognize how extraordinary it is that your heart never faltered, even when you were submerged in the trenches of your deepest pain? And can you let the end of this chapter lead you to a beautiful new beginning? Allow yourself to keep believing in the hope that tomorrow brings; know with every fragment of your being that you are worthy of that.

I **courageously** follow my dreams, even when it's hard, because I **know** that it is always worth it.

The truth is, it may never get any easier to keep showing up for yourself. Believing in a vision that nobody else can see. Honoring your intuition, even when it pulls you away from what feels safe and comfortable. One day, the seed of the dream that's been planted in your heart will bloom. Then a new seed will be planted, and once again you'll have to take a deep breath, summon your courage, and choose a road that has never been traveled before.

When that day comes, you may not feel any braver or more ready than you do right now. Every time you choose to reach for the unknown, you may feel that same twinge of nervousness, that same lingering uncertainty, that same heart-pounding fear. The reality is that this relationship you're cultivating with your heart's consciousness isn't just a chapter of your life but a lifelong journey. And like any relationship, the connection you're creating with the dream that's been written in your heart requires daily nurturing and attention. You must want it and be willing to fight for it. You must keep choosing it every single day. It's not always going to be an easy road, but in the end, it will be worth it because it will be *yours*. Your life, choices, and journey. Your story. *Yours.* It will be incredible and feel surreal, and your entire life will feel like one big miracle. At times, the journey will be harder than you could have imagined, but the outcomes will be better than you had ever dreamed. And you will know that choosing this path was the greatest gift you could ever give yourself. That you wouldn't take back a single step of the road you've traveled. That every part of this long, magical journey—it was all worth it.

My time is **precious** and invaluable, and I choose to spend it on the things that **matter** to me.

Treat your time like it is the most expensive, most cherished thing you own. Treat it like it is *irreplaceable*. Be intentional with how you choose to allocate your most precious resource. Consciously choose what you focus on and how you expend your daily energy—make sure it supports who you are, who you're becoming, and the life you seek to create for yourself. Maybe what you're choosing to spend your time on today will help you to create a more beautiful tomorrow. Perhaps your time will give you the chance to step closer to your dreams or to take care of the people you love. It's possible the higher purpose behind how you spend your time today is simply to experience pure joy or inner peace in this present moment. Or maybe it's to heal and bring sustenance to your soul. There is no right or wrong answer if *it feels right to you*.

The world will try to pull you into things that you *don't* choose: toxic gossip, futile diversions from your goals, work that is draining and unfulfilling. You are not bound to stay loyal to anything that makes you feel less like *you*. The value of your time is incalculable and immeasurable—don't give it away to anything that doesn't serve your highest good. You might need to spend time today having a hard conversation or setting boundaries. You might need to spend time alone so you can begin to understand what you truly want in life. Spend it on serving your present or future self. Don't allow yourself to be dragged into places and situations that mistreat or misuse your time. Don't let anybody tell you how to devote your most invaluable resource.

Even if things don't work out **exactly** as I hope, I will not give up on what's **important** to me.

Strength of mind, inner resilience, and mental fortitude are built with two simple words: *even if*. You can change your entire life by replacing every single *what if* that's ever crossed your mind with those six letters. *Even if.* You ask yourself, *What if this relationship doesn't work out?* Turn it around. *Even if.* Even if it doesn't work out, it's still worth finding out what it can teach you. Even if it doesn't last, it's still worth the extraordinary moments it might gift you. And even if it does ultimately lead to a broken heart, it's still worth keeping your heart open to real love and honest connection. It's still worth continuing to trust that what is meant for you will arrive with perfect timing—and continuing to believe *you are worthy* of epic, once-in-a-lifetime love.

This is the same for every single thing that's important to you. If something truly matters, then you cannot give up on it, even if the road ahead doesn't unfold exactly the way you hope. Instead of *What if I don't get the job?* tell yourself that even if you don't get it, it's still worth trying. Even if this opportunity isn't meant for you, you know there's something better awaiting up ahead. Consider everything you're worried or nervous about right now. Write down all the *what if*s that keep you stuck and afraid to move forward. Turn them around. *Even if.* What is still worth it, even if it doesn't work out the way you hope? What will you not give up on, even if it takes longer than you thought it would? Choose to fight for what you value most in life, even if it requires every bit of strength you possess. *Even if.* Repeat those two words over and over until they're embedded in your memory so you can continue to stay aligned with what's important to you.

True **abundance** begins within me. I receive and accept abundance through becoming **aware** of all the ways in which it already exists in my life.

You don't earn abundance. You don't gain it from external sources. You don't have to struggle or fight to keep it. It doesn't need to be saved out of fear that it will one day run out. True abundance knows no limits and can never be depleted. Most essentially, true abundance is found *only within you*. If you are only seeking abundance through your sight and touch, you will never find it. And what you *do* find will never be enough. You can experience outward abundance in the form of financial prosperity and still feel like *something is always missing*. The path to abundance is not found through gaining a plethora of external resources and hoping it will fill the hole inside; it can only be unearthed from within.

When you feel fulfilled and whole from the inside, then whatever you receive outside of yourself simply adds to your prosperity—but it is not the *source* of your true wealth. You and your abundance are forever inseparable. It is eternally interwoven with your divine essence. If you want to uncover your deep-rooted abundance, simply try to notice the ways in which it already exists by looking at what you *have* rather than what you lack. Appreciate your life. Take a breath; as you inhale, notice that you're not afraid to exhale. You're not afraid to let this current breath go, because you intuitively know the next will follow. You know that you don't have to cling to your last breath, because *another will come*. You don't have to hoard the air around you, because *it is infinitely available to you in this moment*. That is the essence of abundance. It is always accessible and never concealed. When you nurture and cultivate the seeds of abundant joy, peace, and love inside yourself, the whole world around you blooms in response.

When I let go of what is no longer **meant** for me, I make space for even deeper **connections**, more extraordinary experiences, and better **opportunities** to arrive.

When you feel like life is constantly taking from you, remember that energy cannot be destroyed. Energy always comes back. In another person, place, or job. Another opportunity. The love returns. The happiness returns. The excitement returns. It comes back in another shape, form, or manifestation. Life does not just remove things from your world; it also gives and restores. After the dismantling comes the rebuilding. What is cleared will also be filled. When something is taken, something will also be given. There is always more happening beyond your current scope of vision. So let go of these things that are no longer serving you.

In equal measure to what is being destroyed, the Universe is also working behind the scenes to *create*. Nature works in cycles. Seasons change. The earth spins. The moon contracts and expands. Every breath in is balanced with a breath out, and every dark night is followed by the rising of the sun. There is balance in everything. If you've been in a clearing season, losing and letting go of the life you once knew, know that this is only one part of your cycle. It's not the whole story. Life is not trying to squeeze you until you're empty. It's making space for *more*. For more love or joy. For something deeper and more profound than you've ever experienced before. It may feel like the storm will last forever, but it won't. The storm is here to breathe new life into your story—to clear what you've outgrown and make space for a new chapter. Trust the balance of life. Trust the unfolding of the cycle you're in. Trust in what blooms after the rain.

I **deserve** a lifetime filled with **true** joy and happiness.

Joy. That's what's missing. Too often, your joy is treated as an afterthought. First, you think, you must do the hard things. You must face your fears. You must do the tedious, unglamorous, or uninspired work. There is a job to be done. There is sacrifice. And then there is the long journey of healing, releasing, and unraveling. There is always *something* that demands your attention. Something that becomes your priority. And yes, these *something*s are important parts of your journey, but joy is *something* too. The little pockets of happiness, the things that make you light up from the inside, the experiences that cause your inner child to beam and glow—they are just as worthy and deserving of taking up space in this world.

This is one of the most essential parts of being human—to experience pure happiness and delight in your daily life and share this energy with the people around you. To *be* the joy that makes this world feel a little brighter. You're not here solely to know suffering. You're not here only for the aches and pains. *The Universe wants you to be happy.* It wants you to love this life you get to live. Invite joy to be a companion on your life's journey. What is it that makes you truly happy? The people, the activities, the places—these are your destined matches. These are what deserve your most abundant energy. Is it the music? The poetry? The things you do that feel like *play*? Is it swimming in the ocean? Is it dancing under the moon? What makes your body feel lighter? What makes your soul feel free? Let everything else be formed around what brings true joy to your heart. Don't push these things to the periphery of your life. Make them the centerpiece.

I have **everything** I need within me to create the life I've always **dreamed** of living.

Many lights glow within you, adding up to a shining beam that guides you to your dreams. You have the dream that lives inside your heart and ignites tiny sparks of excitement deep within your bones. Your inner vision paints a picture in your mind's eye and feels inextricably linked to your destined future, pushing you forward. Your intuition guides you on your soul's highest path. You have the courage to take inspired action based on what your inner guidance system tells you. You have the discernment to know when something feels *good* and *right* and when the energy just feels off, even if you can't pinpoint why.

Not only do you have the instincts, but you have the wisdom to make the right choices for yourself, no matter what anyone else tells you. And you can trust your judgment and walk away from anything that does not serve your journey or support your growth. Your intelligence at solving problems and coming up with innovative solutions to turn obstacles into opportunities is undeniable. You have the adaptability to move with the flow of life when it asks you to shift directions and alter your course. You persevere against adversity and your hardest challenges. And you have the companionship of your own deep, everlasting love as you walk your authentic path. Your compassion, kindness, and open heart make you a magnet for life's most incredible miracles. Ultimately, you have everything you need to create a life that you fall in love with more and more every day. All along, the magic you've been searching for has always been within, and you can use it to serve yourself in your pursuit of your dream life.

I am worthy of living a **life** that **feels** calm, serene, and effortlessly **beautiful**.

You've met the version of you who felt like you were on the verge of breaking but had no choice but to be resilient. The one who spent night after dark night walking a lonely path without any signs of light on the horizon. You've had to learn how to heal your own heart and be your own rescuer. To pick yourself back up when there were no helping hands. And you've met the version of you who kept leaning into trust, even when it felt like nothing was working out. Who sometimes wanted to give up entirely—but who, instead, continued and discovered a deep well of inner strength and faith.

You've met the tough, persistent, adaptable version of yourself and have played that part so skillfully for a long, long time. But there's another version of you who you haven't spent as much time with: a version of you who is just as strong but doesn't need to prove it. A version of you who gets to lean into *ease* and who always has time for leisurely morning strolls and nights spent under the stars. This version of you rests, plays, and creates just for fun. This you knows calm and serenity. This version not only gives but receives plentifully—and can trust that *the world won't fall down if you let go*. What would it take for you to begin to step into this version of yourself? Visualize how it would feel to walk through this next chapter of your life with grace, softness, and tranquility. Ask your highest self what you need to know to embrace this version of you fully. And day by day, hour by hour, heartbeat by heartbeat, slowly allow this version of yourself to come forward.

I am stepping into a new **chapter** filled with more **positive** elements than I have ever **known** before.

This next chapter isn't going to look like all the ones before. This chapter is for trusting the wisdom of your heart to guide you in the right direction, even when you can't see the entire path ahead. Use this time to follow your bliss and go *all in* on the things that bring you love, joy, and fulfillment. Say yes to what feels beautiful and honest and true—and say no to anything that doesn't settle *just right* in your bones. Choose faith over doubt and courage over fear. Use this time to nurture your inner peace. Open your heart and let joy and gratitude seep into every corner of your life. Take time to create the most honest and beautiful life you can imagine—and let the Universe surprise you with miracles beyond your wildest dreams. Enjoy the sacred sunsets and meaningful connections, and honor the life-force energy that flows through you. Let what's meant for you land softly on your path and let what's not miss you completely.

As you journey on, know with every cell of your being that you are capable, strong, and *always enough*. Honor the innate magic that flows through you and no longer dim your own radiant light. After all, this chapter is for stepping away from *all that you're not* as you fully and unconditionally embrace *all that you are*. This chapter is the story you were always worthy of telling, and it's also the plot twist you've been waiting for. This chapter is a love letter to your mind, body, and soul. Anchor yourself in peace, gratitude, joy, and trust. And most of all, root yourself in love—*pure, steady, unwavering love*. Step into your newest chapter full to the brim with all that nourishes you and embrace the positivity within and outside of yourself.

Index

About the Author

Zanna Keithley is an author, poet, and social media content creator living in Seattle. She began sharing her writing on Instagram in 2020 and continues to write short prose dedicated to inspiring readers to follow their dreams, trust their intuition, and create beautiful and fulfilling lives. Follow her at @zannakeithley.